Is North Korea a Global Threat?

Debra A. Miller, *Book Editor*

Bruce Glassman, *Vice President*
Bonnie Szumski, *Publisher*
Helen Cothran, *Managing Editor*

GREENHAVEN PRESS
An imprint of Thomson Gale, a part of The Thomson Corporation

Detroit • New York • San Francisco • San Diego • New Haven, Conn.
Waterville, Maine • London • Munich

LIBRARY OF CONGRESS CATALOGING-IN-PUBLICATION DATA

Is North Korea a global threat? / Debra A. Miller, book editor.
   p. cm. — (At issue)
  Includes bibliographical references and index.
  ISBN 0-7377-2324-6 (lib. : alk. paper) — ISBN 0-7377-2325-4 (pbk. : alk. paper)
   1. Terrorism—Korea (North). I. Miller, Debra A. II. At issue (San Diego, Calif.)
  HV6433.K7I577 2005
  355'.03305193—dc22
                                                  2004046014

Printed in the United States of America

Contents

Introduction

In October 2002 North Korea announced to U.S. officials that it had been secretly working on a uranium-enriched nuclear weapons program. This announcement was followed in December 2002 by a statement that North Korea was also restarting plutonium-based nuclear facilities that it had promised to freeze under the Agreed Framework, an agreement it made with the United States in 1994. In January 2003 North Korea officially withdrew from the Nuclear Non-Proliferation Treaty (NPT), an international agreement that committed North Korea not to develop nuclear weapons and to allow inspections of its nuclear sites. This series of events plunged the United States and Asia into an international crisis over how to prevent North Korea's unstable, repressive, and dangerous dictator, Kim Jong Il, from developing nuclear weapons.

North Korea's actions between October 2002 and January 2003 are consistent with the nation's long history of belligerent behavior. North Korea is a Communist protégé of the old Soviet Union and Communist China. It was founded in 1948 with Soviet help after the Korean Peninsula was divided into two countries (Communist North Korea and Democratic South Korea) following World War II. Today it is a small country in big trouble. Due largely to the collapse of its Soviet benefactor in 1991, millions of its people are starving and its economy is in desperate condition. It survives largely on aid from the United Nations (UN) and foreign countries, including the United States. Despite its economic weakness, North Korea has commanded center stage in world politics for decades through its belligerent threats and actions. Indeed, it is North Korea's long history of militarism, isolation, and hostility toward other countries that creates an enormous dilemma for policy makers looking for ways to halt North Korea's nuclear ambitions. North Korea, which diverts its sparse resources into maintaining the world's fifth-largest armed force, has acted aggressively toward its neighbors, particularly South Korea, and has gone back on its word in negotiations and agreements. Given this history, policy makers face a thorny dilemma with seemingly no good options for restraining North Korea.

North Korea's history of militarism

Since its creation, North Korea has maintained a strong military and a hostile stance, particularly toward South Korea, the United States, and Japan. The country's first leader and dictator, Kim Il Sung, set North Korea on this course by adopting policies similar to those of the Communist Soviet Union. This approach emphasized military strength and quickly resulted in North Korea invading South Korea in an effort to reunify the Korean Peninsula by military means—a clear act of aggression that started the Korean War. After the war, Kim Il Sung remained in power for many decades, during which he kept North Korea isolated from the outside world, built up North Korea's military, and implemented a highly nationalistic ideology called *juche*, which emphasizes self-reliance and independence from foreign control.

Since the Korean War, North and South Korea technically have remained in a war stance because, although they signed an armistice, they never agreed on a formal peace treaty. Over the years North Korea has employed spies to infiltrate South Korea, made at least four attempts to assassinate South Korean presidents, built numerous invasion tunnels under the demilitarized zone (the dividing line between North and South Korea), and conducted terrorist attacks against South Korean targets.

Today, Kim Il Sung's son, a brutal and combative dictator named Kim Jong Il, rules North Korea. He has largely continued his father's policies of militarism, but on a grander scale. Since North Korea's economic collapse in the 1990s, Kim Jong Il has become adept at using threats of force and manipulative negotiations to obtain economic aid from other countries. He also has steered North Korea to develop weapons of mass destruction. North Korea now possesses both chemical and biological weapons and at least two nuclear bombs. The country also has developed long-range ballistic missiles capable of delivering these weapons to targets in Asia and the United States. In addition, in order to acquire badly needed revenue, Kim Jong Il has made North Korea the world's major seller of ballistic missiles to unstable and anti-U.S. countries such as Iran and Syria.

North Korea's most recent nuclear threats only continue this pattern. They suggest that North Korea may be seeking to develop a nuclear program that can produce a large volume of nuclear weapons each year. This type of weapons capability would give North Korea great power that could be used for many purposes, none good from the standpoint of the United States and other countries. For example, North Korea could use these weapons offensively against its enemies or simply as a deterrent to prevent countries, such as the United States, from taking military action against it or trying to change its regime. In fact, many suggest that America's 2003 war in Iraq, seeking to end the regime of dictator Saddam Hussein, may have caused North Korea to speed up its nuclear efforts for fear that the United States will attack it next. After all, U.S. president George W. Bush listed North Korea alongside Iraq and Iran as part of what he called the "axis of evil" in January 2002. Others believe that Kim Jong Il has no intention of ever using nuclear weapons and is merely practicing a risky foreign policy of brinksmanship and nuclear blackmail as a means to acquire critical foreign aid and security guarantees. However, the most frightening prospect is that North Korea might begin selling nuclear weapons and technology for profit, in much the same way it has been selling missiles and missile technology for years. Such a development could put nuclear weapons into the hands of terrorists.

The puzzle: how to respond to North Korea's actions

For the United States and other nations seeking to control the proliferation of nuclear weapons, North Korea's history of militarism and threatening actions, together with its pattern of deceit and violation of international agreements, poses difficult policy dilemmas. Experts disagree greatly about whether a carrot or a stick approach, or some combination of the two, should be employed. Carrot approaches, such as negotiations and concessions of economic aid, are problematic because Kim Jong Il has shown he cannot be trusted to abide by such agreements. Even among those who support a diplomatic approach, opinions vary widely on how negotiations could be conducted to ensure that North Korea truly gives up its weapons of mass destruction and missiles. Stick approaches, such as military strikes on nuclear facilities or an Iraq-style attack designed to force regime change, are highly dangerous. Military strikes on such a well-armed country would most certainly be met with a military response. For example, North Korea could be provoked to attack South Korea's capital city of Seoul and kill millions of South Koreans. Furthermore, North Korea has declared that it would consider even nonmilitary measures such as economic restrictions or interdictions of North Korea's trade in weapons an "act of war."

To date, the United States has pursued a multinational negotiation strategy that provides for talks between North Korea, the United States, China, Russia, South Korea, and Japan. However, these negotiations have moved extremely slowly and have made little progress. Whether this approach will ultimately be successful and whether the world will be able to contain Kim Jong Il's thirst for nuclear weapons, remains to be seen.

1

North Korea Has an Active Nuclear Weapons Program

Robert S. Norris, Hans M. Kristensen, and Joshua Handler

Robert S. Norris is a senior research associate with the National Resources Defense Council (NRDC), an environmental action organization, and an expert on nuclear arms control and nonproliferation efforts. Hans M. Kristensen is an associate at the Nautilus Institute, a research and consulting organization that focuses on global security issues, and a consultant to the NRDC on nuclear issues. Joshua Handler is a graduate student at Princeton University and a specialist in disarmament and nuclear weapons.

North Korea has become the world's ninth nuclear power. In October 2002 North Korea admitted to U.S. officials that it had a secret uranium enrichment program. North Korea then decided to restart its plutonium reactor and reprocessing plant and resume construction of two larger reactors. In January 2003 North Korea withdrew from the Nuclear Non-Proliferation Treaty. North Korea probably already has enough processed plutonium to build four to five nuclear bombs. In the future, North Korea potentially could produce many more nuclear weapons each year. North Korea also has an active ballistic missile program to produce longer-range missiles capable of hitting Japan, including U.S. bases in Okinawa. North Korea sells these missiles to countries such

Robert S. Norris, Hans M. Kristensen, and Joshua Handler, "North Korea's Nuclear Program, 2003," *Bulletin of Atomic Scientists*, vol. 59, March/April 2002. Copyright © 2002 by the Educational Foundation for Nuclear Science, Chicago, IL 60637. Reproduced by permission of Bulletin of the Atomic Scientists: The Magazine of Global Security News & Analysis.

as Iran. A nuclear-armed North Korea could trigger an arms race in East Asia. Even worse, North Korea could sell its plutonium and nuclear weapons or technology to other countries or terrorists.

North Korea has apparently become the world's ninth nuclear power. Last November [2002], the CIA [U.S. Central Intelligence Agency] estimated that Pyongyang [the capital of North Korea] has one, perhaps two, nuclear weapons. The North Korean crisis, as it has emerged [in 2003], is an extremely complex affair with implications that could drastically affect Asian security and, by extension, U.S. interests. The confrontation has weakened the Nuclear Non-Proliferation Treaty (NPT) and may send signals to others that obtaining nuclear weapons has geopolitical benefits, especially when facing the United States.

Nuclear weapons on the Korean peninsula

Nuclear weapons and Korea have been entwined for more than 50 years. During the Korean War (1950–1953), the United States threatened several times to use nuclear weapons. After the armistice, U.S. military forces remained in South Korea (the Republic of Korea). The United States began deploying several types of nuclear weapons to the South in January 1958, a time of extensive worldwide U.S. nuclear deployments. Initially, four different kinds of nuclear weapons were introduced with U.S. Army forces in South Korea: the Honest John surface-to-surface missile, the massive 280-millimeter gun, the 8-inch artillery shell, and atomic demolition munitions (ADMs). In March 1958, gravity bombs for aircraft were added. From 1960–1964, five more weapon systems were introduced: Lacrosse and Sergeant ballistic missiles, Nike Hercules surface-to-air missiles, Davy Crockett nuclear bazookas, and 155-millimeter artillery shells. The arsenal in South Korea was at its largest in 1967, with approximately 950 nuclear warheads, of eight types.

By the mid-1980s, only the 8-inch and 155-millimeter artillery shells, ADMs, and gravity bombs remained, and the number of warheads had dropped to about 150. With little fanfare and no formal public announcement, in the fall of 1991 President George H.W. Bush ordered the removal of all the remaining weapons, which was accomplished in 1992.

The fact that North Korea (the Democratic People's Republic of Korea, or DPRK) was threatened with nuclear weapons during the Korean War, and that for decades afterwards U.S. weapons were deployed in the South, may have helped motivate former president Kim Il Sung to launch a nuclear weapons program of his own. With Soviet help, the program began in the 1960s. China also provided various kinds of support over the next two decades, and by the late 1980s success was near. A milestone was reached with the construction of a 5-megawatt electric (MWe) [plutonium-based] reactor that began operating in 1986. More recently, Pakistan has played a substantial role in the progress of North Korea's nuclear program.

The Agreed Framework

On October 21, 1994, North Korea and the United States signed the Agreed Framework to defuse a serious crisis—it had been discovered that the North was not declaring all of the spent fuel that it reprocessed, in violation of the NPT. The agreement's main provisions were: North Korea would freeze and eventually dismantle its [plutonium-based] nuclear program, which would be verified by the International Atomic Energy Agency (IAEA); its graphite-moderated reactors would be replaced with two light-water reactors; it would receive heavy fuel oil for heating and electricity production; political and economic relations would be normalized; and both countries would work toward a nuclear weapons-free Korean peninsula and strengthen the nuclear non-proliferation regime.

For North Korea, another important aspect of the accord was the U.S. pledge to "provide formal assurances to the DPRK against the threat or use of nuclear weapons by the United States," a commitment that it says the United States has not lived up to. While North Korea has failed to fulfill all its obligations, Washington has continued to hold a nuclear sword over it. In March 1997, the chief of U.S. Strategic Command told Congress that just as the United States threatened Iraq with nuclear weapons in 1991, "that same message was passed on to the North Koreans back in 1995." And documents obtained under the Freedom of Information Act show that the air force carried out simulated nuclear strikes against North Korea in 1998.

The North Korea nuclear crisis

The latest crisis erupted in early October 2002, when North Korean officials did not deny charges made by James A. Kelly, the

U.S. Assistant Secretary of State for East Asian and Pacific Affairs, that Pyongyang had a secret uranium enrichment program. According to a June 2002 CIA report, described by Seymour Hersh in the January 27 *New Yorker*, in 1997 Pakistan gave North Korea highspeed centrifuges and how-to data on building and testing a uranium-triggered nuclear weapon. (Pakistan's nuclear weapons are based on a Chinese implosion design that uses a core of highly enriched uranium.) In return, North Korea gave Pakistan missile technology and parts.

> *North Korea is widely believed to have produced and separated enough plutonium for a small number of nuclear warheads.*

After the United States went public with the North Korean program on October 16 [2002], Pyongyang announced its intention to further break its commitment to the Agreed Framework and restart its 5-MWe reactor and reprocessing plant and resume construction of two larger reactors. In December [2002], it removed the IAEA safeguard seals at the nuclear research center in Yongbyon, shut down the monitoring cameras, and ordered the IAEA inspectors out of the country.

On January 10 [2003], this fast-moving train of events culminated in Pyongyang's announcement that North Korea would withdraw from the NPT—the only country ever to do so. According to the *New York Times* (January 31), U.S. satellites detected activity in North Korea throughout January that appeared to indicate it was removing its spent nuclear fuel rods from storage.

North Korea's nuclear program

The center of North Korea's nuclear program is at Yongbyon, some 60 miles north of Pyongyang. Its major facilities include the 5-MWe reactor and reprocessing plant that it has threatened to restart, as well as a fuel fabrication plant. The construction of a 50-MWe reactor in Yongbyon was halted under the 1994 agreement, as was construction of a 200-MWe reactor in Taechon. North Korea has uranium deposits estimated at 26 million tons and is thought to have one active uranium mine.

North Korea is widely believed to have produced and separated enough plutonium for a small number of nuclear warheads. Most or all of the plutonium came from the 5-MWe reactor at Yongbyon, which went critical on August 14, 1985, and became operational the following January. The U.S. intelligence community believes that during a 70-day shutdown in 1989, North Korea secretly removed fuel from the reactor and separated the plutonium. Estimates vary as to how much plutonium was obtained. The State Department believes about 6–8 kilograms; the CIA and Defense Intelligence Agency say 8–9 kilograms, an estimate consistent with the careful analysis of the Institute for Science and International Security. South Korean, Japanese, and Russian analysts have made much higher estimates, ranging up to 24 kilograms.

North Korea has never admitted it possesses nuclear weapons, but it appears likely that it does. *Nucleonics* and *NBC Nightly News* reported in 1993 that reprocessed plutonium had already been converted from a liquid form to metal, and several U.S. officials concluded that Pyongyang had made it into a bomb. In November 2002, the CIA went further than its previous estimates, stating, "The United States has been concerned about North Korea's desire for nuclear weapons and has assessed since the early 1990s that the North has one or possibly two weapons using plutonium it produced prior to 1992."

Very little is known about North Korea's uranium enrichment program. Questions about it include: How many centrifuges (used to enrich uranium) does North Korea have, and where are they located? Has it begun enriching uranium? If so, what level is the uranium enriched to, how much has been enriched, and how much will be? Hersh reported that the CIA concluded that the North began to enrich uranium in significant quantities in 2001. Analysts at the Nonproliferation Policy Education Center estimate its future production rate could be anywhere from 40–100 kilograms a year.

North Korea's bomb-making capabilities

The precise amount of plutonium (or uranium) needed for a bomb depends on the technical capabilities of scientists and engineers as well as the desired yield. With 1 kilogram of plutonium, designers with high technical capabilities could make a bomb with a 1 kiloton yield; with 3 kilograms, a 20-kiloton yield. Designers with low technical skills would need 3 kilograms for a 1-kiloton yield, and 6 kilograms for a 20-kiloton yield (see table). The Trinity test and the Nagasaki (Fat Man) bomb each used 6.1 kilograms of plutonium and produced yields of approximately 21 kilotons.

No one knows for sure what the skill level of North Korean bomb designers is, but a medium capability seems possible. For weapons production, this might mean that for a lower-yield weapon (1–5 kilotons) they would need around 2 kilograms of plutonium, and for a higher-yield weapon (10–20 kilotons) approximately 3 kilograms. Assuming that North Korea has a medium capability, 8–9 kilograms of plutonium might be enough for four or five weapons. During the crisis in 1994, then-Defense Secretary William Perry said, "If they had a very advanced technology, they could make five bombs out of the amount of plutonium we estimate they have."

The potential size of North Korea's future arsenal is unsettling. The CIA estimates that the 50-MWe reactor at Yongbyon and the 200-MWe reactor at Taechon would generate about 275 kilograms of plutonium per year (operating at full capacity), but it would take several years to complete the reactors. Forty kilograms of highly enriched uranium would be enough to produce six to 10 low-yield nuclear weapons or four or five higher-yield weapons per year.

North Korea could make more bombs if it uses a composite-core design (a smaller plutonium sphere encased in a shell of highly enriched uranium) than if it builds designs that use only plutonium or only uranium. A few days after the Trinity test of July 16, 1945, the United States considered using some or all of the highly enriched uranium intended for Little Boy in order to increase the number of available bombs, but rejected the idea. The U.S. successfully tested the design in Operation Sandstone during the spring of 1948.

Ballistic missiles

North Korea has a very active ballistic missile program, carefully documented by Joseph S. Bermudez Jr. in a 1999 report published by the Center for Nonproliferation Studies. Beginning in the 1960s, the Soviet Union supplied various types of missiles, supporting technologies, and training to North Korea. China began supplying North Korea with missile technology in the 1970s. In 1979 or 1980, Egypt supplied Pyongyang with a small number of Soviet Scud B missiles, along with launchers and support equipment. North Korea reverse-engineered the Scud and built an industrial infrastructure to produce its own missiles, eventually at a rate of eight to 10 per month in 1987 and 1988. It sold approximately 100 to Iran, many of which were fired at Iraqi cities during the Iran-Iraq War. An extended-range version of the missile, known as the Scud C, was first test-launched in June 1990. Its 500-kilometer range was achieved mainly by reducing the payload from 1,000 to 770 kilograms. It is estimated that a total of 600–1,000 Scud B and Cs were produced by the end of 1999. Half of them were sold to foreign countries.

> *The Bush administration's hope that North Korea will give up its nuclear program seems fanciful at this point.*

Driven by a desire for longer missile ranges, North Korea developed what is known in the West as the Nodong (or Rodong), which has a range of 1,350–1,500 kilometers (depending upon payload) and is capable of hitting Japan and U.S. bases in Okinawa. Nodongs were deployed in the mid-1990s, with nearly 100 fielded and another 50 or so sold to foreign countries. The missile is known as the Ghauri I in Pakistan and the Shahab 3 in Iran. North Korea wants a missile with an intercontinental range, and work is under way to achieve it. The two-stage Taepodong-1 is intended to carry a 1,000–1,500 kilogram warhead to a range of 1,500–2,500 kilometers. A three-stage space-launch version, intended to place a DPRK satellite in orbit, was launched on August 31, 1998, from the facility at Musudan-ri. The missile flew over Japan, causing much consternation. Its first and second stages separated and landed in the water, but the third stage, after traveling more than 5,500 kilometers (3,450 miles), broke up and the satellite did not reach orbit.

The longer-range Taepodong-2 may be ready for flight-testing. Depending on the payload, it may have a range greater than 6,000 kilometers, sufficient to strike parts of Hawaii and Alaska.

It is reasonable to assume that North Korea wants to put nuclear warheads on its ballistic missiles, but whether it has achieved this capability is unknown. Other countries that have developed nuclear weapons usually chose airplanes as their initial delivery method, followed in most instances by the development of ballistic missiles of various ranges. North Korea is an exception to this pattern—ballistic missiles are its preferred delivery method, and aircraft do not appear to have a role.

The North's closed society and the covert nature of its nuclear program make it a "difficult intelligence collection target," as the CIA puts it. No one knows what North Korea's nuclear intentions are—Pyongyang relies heavily on ambiguity in all that it does. Has [President] Kim Jong Il decided that North Korea's security requires a stockpile of nuclear weapons? Or are its actions and words another instance of its strange brand of bargaining with the United States, in which North Korea offers to make concessions in exchange for diplomatic recognition, non-aggression pacts, money, or goods? It may be that, after 30 years of offensive U.S. nuclear posturing on the peninsula and being recently labeled as part of an "axis of evil," Pyongyang is simply ready to play hardball. (Other factors that probably affected North Korea's actions include the Bush administration's new National Security Strategy, which makes preemptive strikes a priority.)

The Bush administration's hope that North Korea will give up its nuclear program seems fanciful at this point. What incentives could possibly be offered that would cause it to give up its weapons program, dismantle its nuclear complex, and agree to an intrusive verification regime? It is highly unlikely that North Korea will agree to abandon the very thing that gives it leverage with its neighbors and the United States.

A nuclear-armed North Korea could trigger an arms race in East Asia and beyond. It could harden the U.S. posture toward North Korea and reinvigorate the extended nuclear deterrence strategies in the region. Worse, Japan might decide to undertake a nuclear weapons program of its own, which would surely provoke a Chinese response, which in turn could cause reverberations in India and Pakistan. There could also be repercussions in Taiwan and South Korea, both of which had fledgling nuclear weapons programs of their own before U.S. pressure forced their termination.

Perhaps the larger danger: North Korea could sell its plutonium, highly enriched uranium, or finished weapons to other countries or terrorists. Its track record with ballistic missiles is not encouraging. It has made missile deals with Iran, Yemen, Syria, and Pakistan—lucrative sources of income to the impoverished country. Fissile material and nuclear weapons would be even more lucrative.

2

North Korea Is Not a Nuclear Threat

David C. Kang

David C. Kang is an associate professor of government at Dartmouth College, an adjunct fellow at the Center for National Policy, and a senior fellow at the Korean Institute for International Studies in Seoul. He is the author of Crony Capitalism: Corruption and Development in South Korea and the Philippines.

North Korea's leader Kim Jong Il is a brutal and repressive dictator who allows North Koreans to die of starvation while building a massive military machine. Many people fear that if he acquires nuclear weapons, North Korea might invade South Korea or even attack the United States. However, North Korea is not really a serious military threat because for the last fifteen years it has declined both economically and militarily. Today, South Korea's military is better equipped and better trained than North Korea's military. In addition, South Korea is supported by massive U.S. military forces. Given its relative weakness, North Korea does not intend to start a war; the purpose of its army and fierce rhetoric is to deter a U.S. attack. It is acquiring nuclear weapons and missiles for similar deterrence purposes. North Korea will not use its nuclear weapons offensively because that would be suicide, and North Korea's actions indicate it wants to survive.

North Korean leader Kim Jong-il is a brutal dictator who has impoverished a nation in order to sustain a massive mili-

David C. Kang, "Threatening, but Deterrence Works," *Nuclear North Korea: A Debate on Engagement Strategies,* by Victor D. Cha and David C. Kang. New York: Columbia University Press, 2003. Copyright © 2003 by Columbia University Press, 61 W. 62nd St., New York, NY 10023. All rights reserved. Reproduced by permission.

tary machine. He presides over horrifying human rights abuses and concentration camps. Due to its bungled economic policies, as many as one million North Koreans may have died from starvation in the past decade. Kim Jong-il is a reclusive, enigmatic, callous, and, some say, irrational leader. How can such a man—and such a country—have any legitimate security concerns? Shouldn't the United States and the rest of the world fear such unpredictable behavior? Isn't North Korea responsible for its own dilemma? Indeed, if North Korea does develop a nuclear weapon, wouldn't that be the worst possible outcome—a madman with a huge gun?

These are not new concerns. Ever since the first Korean War in 1950, scholars and policymakers have been predicting a second one, started by an invasion from the North. Even in 1997, the Defense Intelligence Agency still considered a Korean war to be the primary near-term military concern of the United States, and the most recent worry is that North Korea may develop nuclear weapons, and perhaps even engage in a missile attack on the United States. . . .

North Korea's perspective

Yet for fifty years North Korea has not come close to starting a war.

This raises a question: is North Korea as dangerous as is popularly believed?

Although accurate, the description of North Korea [as repressive and militant] is incomplete. Just as important to any complete picture of North Korea in 2003 is how weak it really is. In the past 15 years, the balance of power has shifted dramatically against the North. North Korea is also a tiny country that has lost its allies and faces a threatening United States. The state of New Hampshire's economy is twice as large as that of North Korea, while South Korea's economy is thirty times larger. The United States is openly belligerent toward it. . . . With the recently announced National Security Strategy that moves the U.S. toward a stated policy of preemptive strikes, the North is worried that if it agrees to disarm and abandon its deterrent posture, the United States will move to destroy it. The North deters preemptive action by the U.S. precisely because the costs of a war on the peninsula are staggeringly high. North Korea's threatening rhetoric and large army exist to deter the U.S. and convince the U.S. that the costs of war are too high.

This raises another question: does North Korea have legitimate security fears?

In a nutshell, the problem is this: the United States refuses to give security guarantees to North Korea until it proves it has dismantled its weapons program. The North refuses to disarm until it has security guarantees from the United States.

> *North Korea's threatening rhetoric and large army exist to deter the U.S. and convince the U.S. that the costs of war are too high.*

Hence, stalemate.

The key issue is whether North Korea has legitimate security concerns. If it does—and I will argue that this is the case— we can explain the pattern of North Korean behavior and also point to a solution. North Korea's nuclear weapons, missile programs, and massive conventional military deployments are aimed at deterrence and defense. If North Korea really wanted to develop nuclear weapons for offensive purposes, it would have done so long ago. Even if the North develops nuclear weapons, it will not use them because of a devastating U.S. response. The North wants a guarantee of security from the U.S., and a policy of pressure will only make North Korea feel even more insecure. Even isolation is at best a holding measure, while economic sanctions—or even economic engagement alone—will be unlikely to get North Korea to abandon its weapons program.

Without movement toward resolving the security fears of the North, progress in resolving the nuclear weapons issue will be limited. The United States and North Korea are still technically at war—the 1953 armistice was never replaced with a peace treaty. The U.S. has been unwilling to discuss even a nonaggression pact, much less a peace treaty or normalization of ties. With the U.S. calling North Korea a terrorist nation and [U.S. secretary of defense] Donald Rumsfeld discussing the possibility of war, it is no surprise that North Korea feels threatened. Upon closer examination, North Korea never had the material capabilities to be a serious contender to the U.S.-ROK [Republic of Korea, the formal name for South Korea] alliance, and it quickly fell further behind. So the real question has not been whether North Korea would prevent or preempt as South Korea caught up, but instead why North Korea might fight as it fell farther and farther behind. . . .

If North Korea was so weak, why did so many people conclude that North Korea was the likely instigator of war? Since North Korea was not powerful, scholars and policymakers hypothesized extreme psychological tendencies to North Korean leaders. That is, if the material conditions such as military or economic power did not lead logically to a conclusion of North Korean threat, then the leadership's psychology was what must matter. These ancillary and *ad hoc* psychological assumptions range from an irrational North Korean leadership to an extremely strong preference for invasion. Most theories of war focus on material conditions such as relative power, but in the case of North Korea, the real analytic lifting has been done by psychological assumptions about intent. As I will show, none of these assumptions are tenable.

The U.S. military has deterred North Korea

The explanation for a half-century of stability and peace on the Korean peninsula is actually quite simple: deterrence works. Since 1953 North Korea has faced both a determined South Korean military, and more importantly, U.S. military deployments that at their height comprised 100,000 troops and more than 100 nuclear-tipped Lance missiles aimed at North Korea. Even today the United States maintains bases in South Korea that include 38,000 troops, nuclear-capable airbases, and naval facilities that guarantee U.S. involvement in any conflict on the peninsula. While in 1950 there might have been reason for confidence in the North, the war was disastrous for the Communists, and without massive Chinese involvement North Korea would have ceased to exist. Even during the cold war, North Korea's leadership never challenged this deterrence on the peninsula. As I will show, the attempted assassinations of South Korea's authoritarian leaders during the 1970s and 1980s have stopped because they would be clearly counterproductive in a democratic South Korea, and will not begin again. Given the tension on the peninsula, small skirmishes have had the potential to spiral out of control, yet these incidents on the peninsula have been managed with care on both sides. The peninsula has been stable for fifty years because deterrence has been clear and unambiguous.

The end of the cold war marked a major change in North Korea's security position. The past 15 years have seen the balance of power turn sharply against the North. What was stable deterrence during the cold war by both sides has swung quickly in favor of the West and South Korea. In the 1990s North Korea lost its two cold war patrons, experienced economic and environmental crises, and fell far behind the South. Although during the cold war the North was the aggressor, this shift in power put it on the defensive. It was only when the balance began to turn against the North that it began to pursue a nuclear weapons program. Both the weapons program and the bellicose nature of its rhetoric are an attempt to continue to deter the U.S. from taking any preemptive moves against it.

North Korea has the worst public relations in the world. The North's anachronistic cold war rhetoric and seeming inability to present itself reasonably make it difficult for even impartial people in the West to make sense of its actions. As history has shown, pressure only exacerbates North Korean security fears. Since North Korea does not pose the threat many analysts think it does, the United States may be wasting resources aimed at the North, and may also be unnecessarily raising tensions throughout the region.

I want to emphasize that I am neither defending nor justifying North Korean behavior. Much of the regime's actions are abhorrent and morally indefensible. However, sound foreign policy is built upon clear and objective analysis of the conditions at hand. Emotion and ideology have often interfered with the reasoned study of North Korea, and this has led scholars and policymakers to consistently overestimate the North Korean threat and to misunderstand the motivations behind North Korea's actions. . . .

Why North Korea is not a military threat

In explaining North Korea's foreign policy, a useful place to begin is by exploring why North Korea has become weaker and what has deterred it from starting a war. North Korea chose not to attack the South during the cold war, even though it was at the height of its power and was supported by the PRC [People's Republic of China] and the Soviet Union. The past 15 years have led to severe economic and military decline in North Korea, and it is now much weaker than South Korea. . . .

South Korea has always had twice the population of the

North. In economic terms, North Korea was never as large as the South, and even at its closest was no more than three-quarters the size of the South. North Korea was never close to the South in absolute size, and indeed after 1960 rapidly began falling farther and farther behind. North Korea's GNP [gross national product] in 1960 was $1.52 billion, while South Korea's GNP was $1.95 billion. By 1970 North Korea had grown to $3.98 billion, while in the South GNP was $7.99 billion.

> *The North's anachronistic cold war rhetoric and seeming inability to present itself reasonably make it difficult for even impartial people in the West to make sense of its actions.*

On a per capita income basis the North was never much farther ahead of the South, either. The North and South were roughly equivalent until the mid-1970s, when the South began to rapidly leave the North behind. In 1960 North Korea's per capita GNP was $137 as compared to $94 in the South, and in 1970 the North's per capita income was $286 to $248 in the South. However, by 1980 the North's income was $758 per capita, while the South's was $1,589, and by 1990 $1,065 to $5,569. Furthermore, in terms of preventive war, per capita income is not as important as absolute size, because small nations may be rich on a per capita basis (Singapore, Switzerland) but be militarily insignificant.

In terms of defense spending, North Korea quickly fell behind the South, spending less on defense by the mid-1970s. As far back as 1977 the South was spending more than the North on defense in absolute dollar terms, $1.8 billion in the South opposed to $1 billion by the North. The only measure by which the North outspent the South was on a per-capita GNP basis, which is an indicator of weakness, not strength. Additionally these numbers do not include military transfers from their respective patrons. Between 1965 and 1982 North Korea received $1.5 billion in military transfers, mostly from the Soviet Union. Over the same time period South Korea received $5.1 billion from the United States.

Thus the most common measures of power in international relations—economic size and defense spending—show quite clearly that North Korea was never larger than South Korea, has been smaller on an absolute and per-capita basis than the South for at least 30 years, and continues to fall farther behind. Those who see North Korea as threatening need to explain why North Korea—having waited 50 years—would finally attack now that it is one-twentieth the size of the South.

In military capabilities the North and South Korea were in rough parity for the first two decades following the Korean War (1950–53), and then the North began to fall behind. . . . Most interesting is that North Korea did not begin its massive expansion of its armed forces until well into the 1970s. This is most probably a response to its falling further behind the South. But for the past 30 years, North Korea's training, equipment, and overall military quality has steadily deteriorated relative to the South.

The South Korean military is better-equipped, better-trained, and more versatile with better logistics and support than the North Korean military, and some assessments suggest that this may double combat effectiveness. Although the military has continued to hold pride of place in the North Korean economy, there have been increasing reports of reduced training due to the economic problems. *Foong-Ang Ilbo*, one of South Korea's major daily newspapers, quoted an unidentified Defense Ministry official as saying that North Korea's air force had made 100 training sorties per day in 1996, down from 300 to 400 before the end of 1995, and that the training maneuvers of ground troops had also been reduced to a "minimum level." American military officials have noted that individual North Korean pilots take one training flight per month, compared with the 10 flights per month that U.S. pilots take. This drastically degrades combat readiness.

> *❝ The past 15 years have led to severe economic and military decline in North Korea, and it is now much weaker than South Korea. ❞*

The bulk of North Korea's main battle tanks are of 1950s vintage, and most of its combat aircraft were introduced before 1956. Evaluations after the [1990–1991] Gulf War concluded that Western weaponry is at least twice, or even four-times, better than older Soviet-vintage systems. By the 1990s North Korea's military was large in absolute numbers but the quality of their forces was severely degraded relative to South Korea's and the U.S. military. [Scholar] Michael O'Hanlon notes that: "Given the obsolescence of most North Korean equipment, however, actual capabilities of most forces would be notably less than raw numbers suggest. About half of North Korea's major weapons are of roughly 1960s design; the other half are even older."

To view the North as superior in military terms is a mistake. But even more surprising about many of these accounts is that they measure the strength of the North Korean military only against that of the ROK, without including the U.S. forces, either present in Korea or those potential reinforcements. North Korea knows that it would fight the United States as well as the South, and it is wishful thinking to hope that the North Korean military planners are so naïve as to ignore the U.S. military presence in South Korea, expecting the U.S. to pack up and go home if the North invaded. Comparisons between the South and the North that ignore the role of the United States are seriously misleading as to the real balance of power on the peninsula.

> *North Korea is not a threat to start an unprovoked war.*

In event of a full-scale conflict, the United States could reinforce the peninsula with overwhelming power. Currently 36,000 U.S. troops are stationed in Korea, including the U.S. Second infantry division and 90 combat aircraft including 72 F-16s. In addition, 36,000 troops are stationed in Japan, including the headquarters of the Seventh fleet at Yokosuka naval base, 14,000 Marines, and 90 combat aircraft. This is only the beginning, as more would soon arrive from within the United States.

This economic and military comparison of North and South Korea shows that North Korea never had a lead over the South, and after the 1960s quickly began falling behind. The end of the cold war marked the beginning of a major change in North Korea's fortunes, as North Korea continued to have economic difficulties, while its allies deserted it. This situation has only become more grave in the new millennium.

North Korea is not a threat to start an unprovoked war.

North Korea was never in a preeminent position relative to the South, and the real question for the pessimists is why they continue to believe that a nation that is far behind and falling farther behind might still attack. The weak may attack the strong—but the conditions under which we expect that to happen do not exist on the peninsula. Yet many people still see the situation as tense and threatening. This is true, but it is true because deterrence at its heart requires both sides to know that the other side can severely damage it. . . .

North Korea's nuclear weapons

The world has become alarmed in recent years not because of the North's conventional military forces, but rather because it is pursuing a nuclear weapons program combined with a ballistic missile program. The real American fear of the past decade has been that a nuclear-armed North Korea might potentially strike targets even in the United States itself. However, these weapons also serve a deterrent function. Given the weakness of North Korea compared to the South and the U.S., and their security fears that arise from that weakness, it is not surprising that the North seeks security assurances from the United States. Deterrence also means that North Korea will not use its weapons—if it actually develops them—for offensive purposes. The consequences would be annihilation by the U.S.

For deterrence to be stable, it requires an adequate level of force to make an attack senseless, but cannot tip over into a level or type of capabilities that would make pre-emption tempting to the other side. Would the acquisition of nuclear weapons by North Korea be destabilizing to the balance of power on the peninsula? The logic of deterrence theory would argue "no," because North Korea would still be deterred by the overwhelming conventional and military power of the United States.

As the tragic events of September 2001 demonstrate, no missile shield will protect a nation against determined terrorist attacks. Yet North Korea has not engaged in terrorism for well over a decade, because their goal is not suicide and random wanton destruction, but survival. As to North Korea's missile program, this is part of their deterrence strategy. North Korea could blow up terrorist bombs in downtown Seoul or Tokyo (or Washington, D.C.) every week if they wanted to. As for rogue states and their alleged plans to fire a couple of nuclear warheads at the United States, there are three basic reasons to doubt this threat. First, North Korea has not yet developed this capability—it is only feared that eventually they may do so. Second, to actually use nuclear weapons would be suicide, since any attack on the U.S. would result in massive American retaliation, and North Korea's efforts over the past decade show that it has an intense desire to survive. Finally, why develop an expensive ballistic missile to shoot at the United States when it would be so much easier just to smuggle in a nuclear weapon? There is a difference between capabilities and intentions—while missiles will not give North Korea any more terrorist capability than they already possess, they do provide a much stronger military deterrent than could terrorist bombings.

> *North Korea cannot hope to win a war against the United States. Therefore, if the U.S. commitment to the South remains strong the likelihood of war on the peninsula is slight.*

I have two points about nuclear tensions in Korea. First, two or three crude nuclear weapons provide no offensive capability and would not significantly alter the military balance on the peninsula, although the diplomatic context may change. North Korea will be no more likely to win a war with nuclear weapons than without them. North Korea, knowing that the stakes are even greater, and that the United States could respond with nuclear weapons, might even be less likely to launch a war. Nuclear weapons confer no offensive capability. Nuclear weapons are too large and powerful to be able to confer militarily useful offensive capability. Nuclear weapons do not "fight" anything, they merely destroy. And thus they offer little offensive or defensive capability. What nuclear weapons do best is deter, for they allow the loser of a war to kill the winner. Nuclear weapons hold little offensive value, but were North Korea to develop the bomb, North Korea would have a robust deterrent. . . .

Second, robust deterrence on the Korean peninsula has resulted from a steadfast U.S. commitment to the South. Less important to deterrence than actual American troops stationed on the peninsula is the potential U.S. involvement. North Korea cannot hope to win a war against the United States. Therefore, if the U.S. commitment to the South remains strong the likelihood of war on the peninsula is slight.

Nuclear weapons are political, not military, instruments. Their value is far greater unused than deployed and delivered. Particularly if North Korea has a tiny stockpile of weapons (one or two), they would do virtually nothing that conventional weapons cannot already do. North Korea already has the conventional capability to destroy Seoul. North Korea can already target the Japanese islands with their Scud missiles.

There is only one difference that would occur from using nuclear weapons: their deployment would remove any barriers on the part of the U.S. and South Korea for a limited war. "The gloves would come off," with no limit to the escalation the U.S. could bring. Virtually any domestic constraint in the United States against using nuclear weapons or overwhelming force would most likely vanish, and the result would undoubtedly be the destruction of the North Korean regime.

The main difference between North Korea and [terrorist] Osama bin Laden is that we know exactly where North Korea is. And, were they to launch a missile, we would know exactly who fired it from the minute it was fired, and know exactly where to aim our retaliatory strikes. This is a major difference, and a major deterrent to nation-states when they consider the use of force.

Whether the goal was a bargaining chip or an effective deterrent, the pursuit of nuclear weapons by North Korea should come as no surprise. As [professor] Andrew Mack writes, "From the North Korean perspective, the reasons for not going nuclear may be outweighed by the perception of a growing strategic need for nuclear weapons." Their allies have deserted them. North Korea has a stagnant and crumbling economic infrastructure. The U.S. is threatening to them. In 1990, North Korea's Foreign Minister Kim Yong-Nam, said that détente between the Soviet Union and South Korea ". . . will leave us no other choice but to take measures to provide us for ourselves [sic] some weapons for which we have so far relied on the Soviet Union."

3

North Korea Is a Terrorist Threat

John Larkin, Donald Macintyre, and Nick Papadopoulos

John Larkin, Donald Macintyre, and Nick Papadopoulos are reporters for Time International.

It is no secret that North Korea is selling missiles abroad. At least half a dozen countries, including Pakistan, Libya, and Syria, are known to have bought the missiles. However, U.S. officials have become increasingly concerned that North Korea, in its desperation to prop up its failing economy, is also selling nuclear weapons technology to rogue states. The United States seeks to uncover and stop the proliferation of North Korean weaponry—perhaps even through a naval and aerial blockade of North Korea. This strategy, however, is risky because North Korea has threatened to attack South Korea if economic sanctions are imposed. In addition, international maritime law makes it extremely difficult to stop ships on the high seas. Weapons trade is also hard to stop because it is impossible to tell whether "dual-use" material will be used for weapons or peaceful purposes. The success of the strategy will ultimately depend on the cooperation of North Korea's two traditional allies: China and Russia.

Sunan Airport on the outskirts of North Korea's capital city, Pyongyang, is one of the world's bleaker transportation hubs, a collection of featureless concrete buildings distinguished only by a giant portrait of North Korean leader Kim

John Larkin, Donald Macintyre, and Nick Papadopoulos, "Arsenal of the Axis: North Korea Already Supplies the Missiles to Rogue States. Now It Poses a New Threat: Nuclear Proliferation," *Time International,* July 14, 2003. Copyright © 2003 by Time, Inc. Reproduced by permission.

Jong Il gazing beatifically over shabby tarmac. Though unpicturesque, Sunan has been providing U.S. spy satellites with plenty of photo opportunities of late. On at least six occasions between April and early July [2003], satellites spotted Iranian IL-76 cargo planes being loaded with wooden crates at Sunan. The frequency of the flights was unusual—normally no more than two flights a year take off from Sunan bound for Iran, according to U.S. government sources. But of greater concern was the size and shape of the crates, which indicated their contents. "It was cruise missiles," says an official in the Bush Administration. So sure was Washington of the jets' cargo that a complaint was lodged with China, which had allowed the flights to traverse its airspace to reach Iran.

That North Korea is selling arms abroad is no revelation. At least half a dozen countries—including Pakistan, Libya and Syria—are known to have purchased missiles from the rogue regime. But analysts and hard-liners in the U.S. are increasingly concerned that a desperate North Korea is spreading more than conventional arms—it is bartering its atomic weapons technology to Iran, creating an unholy, and far more dangerous, alliance between the two other members of President George W. Bush's "axis of evil." "If I send a shipment of missile components on a plane, it doesn't mean I can't send with it a nuclear scientist with a hard drive," says Joseph Bermudez, a widely respected senior analyst at Jane's Information Group. Asserts Yossef Bodansky, director of the U.S. Congressional Task Force on Terrorism and Unconventional Warfare: "We know there is cooperation between North Korea and Iran in the nuclear field. The Iranians have a very comprehensive military nuclear program, and North Korea has been crucial in that." He cites Middle East intelligence sources that indicate the collaboration began in the mid-1990s.

Iran says its nuclear program is for peaceful power generation only. To ensure that is the case, the International Atomic Energy Agency (IAEA) along with the U.S. and the European Union are pressing Iran's leaders to sign an additional protocol to the Nuclear Nonproliferation Treaty that would allow tougher IAEA inspections. There's no solid evidence in the public domain to indicate that Iran is chasing the Bomb—and in the aftermath of the debacle over Iraq's still-undiscovered weapons of mass destruction, it's impossible to conclude that the U.S. intelligence community has an abundance of secret knowledge of the Iran–North Korea partnership or that U.S.

government officials are correctly interpreting it.

Evidence is mounting, however, and not all of it is emanating from Bush Administration hard-liners. The National Council of Resistance of Iran (NCRI), a Paris-based Iranian dissident group, claims that North Korean scientists have been helping Iran build a nuclear facility that could be used to produce bomb-making material. [In December 2002], NCRI blew the whistle on Iran's uranium-enrichment plant in Natanz, heightening international concern about the nature of Tehran's nuclear ambitions. Just how much nuclear help Iran is getting from North Korea isn't clear, says NCRI spokesman Alireza Jafarzadeh. "We do know they have benefited," he says.

> *That North Korea is selling arms abroad is no revelation. At least half a dozen countries—including Pakistan, Libya and Syria—are known to have purchased missiles from the rogue regime.*

The U.S. is seeking additional proof—and is stepping up the pressure. [In July 2003] the U.S. State Department issued sanctions against a North Korean company, Changgwang Sinyong, along with five Chinese companies for selling arms technology to Iran [in 2002]. Meanwhile, *Time* has learned that U.S. Under Secretary of State for Arms Control and International Security John Bolton traveled to the Middle East [in June 2003] in part to persuade several Arab nations to share intelligence with the U.S. on any suspicious traffic between Iran and North Korea. A U.S. official familiar with the trip says Middle Eastern diplomats are "concerned about North Korea exporting nuclear technology, know-how or fissile material to the region."

Analysts cite mutual interests that Iran and North Korea share as reason to suspect the two countries are collaborating. Intelligence sources say North Korea is working its way up the ladder of nuclear sophistication by acquiring the ability to make not just crude, clumsy A-bombs but also warheads small enough to fit atop its missile arsenal—and Pyongyang has already warned it would be willing to sell its expertise and nuclear material unless the U.S. delivers aid and security guarantees.

Arms sales are one of North Korea's few sources of hard currency to prop up its dysfunctional economy. Since the U.S. cut off oil shipments [in 2002] in an effort to pressure Kim to abandon his nukes, the North is also desperately short of fuel to keep electrical generators running and its ramshackle manufacturing economy ticking over. Analysts note that Iran has plenty of oil to trade for arms—along with a strong desire to acquire nuclear weapons, according to Bush administration hawks.

Uncovering and halting the proliferation of North Korean military hardware—perhaps even through a naval and aerial blockade—has become a key component of U.S. efforts to contain the nuclear threat. On his swing through the Middle East, Bolton made it clear to his hosts that the U.S. expected support for a plan to interdict North Korean arms shipments in the air and on the high seas. The controversial plan was first aired during a mid-June [2003] meeting in Madrid between representatives of 11 countries: the U.S., Australia, Canada, France, Germany, Italy, Japan, the Netherlands, Poland, Portugal and Spain. North Korea's arms sales "finance their nuclear weapons program," says Bolton. "This is not money that goes to the starving people of North Korea."

But cordoning off the North presents legal and practical difficulties. One such obstacle: stopping ships on the high seas is questionable under international maritime law. The interception and boarding of a North Korean freighter in the Arabian Sea last December [2002] by Spanish patrol boats was not legally kosher, says a Western diplomat, despite the fact that the ship was found to be carrying North Korean-made Scud missiles to Yemen. The freighter was allowed to continue to its destination. Such interdictions will be "legally extremely complex, or just flat-out impossible," says the diplomat. However, a senior Bush Administration official says a proposed resolution before the U.N. Security Council might provide the cover needed to intercept shipments of missiles, which currently are legal to sell under international law. Even with wide-ranging support, stopping North Korea's arms traffic is dangerous. Pyongyang has repeatedly threatened to attack South Korea if economic sanctions are imposed. In a typically bellicose statement sent to the U.N. Security Council on June 27 [2003] North Korea warned that U.S.-backed sanctions or blockades would "return the Korean peninsula to a state of war."

Nevertheless, ports around the globe are under U.S. pressure to tighten lax export controls that allow North Korea to source much of the high-tech machinery and parts it needs to build conventional arms—as well as weapons of mass destruction.

Following revelations [in 2003] that some Japanese-based companies had exported items to the North that could have been used to build atom bombs, Japan has attempted to curtail some of its trade with the regime. On May 8 [2003], for example, Tokyo police raided a trading company called Meishin, which is run by members of Japan's North Korean community. Police accused Meishin of exporting transformers whose workaday function of regulating electrical current could have had useful applications in Pyongyang's uranium-enrichment program.

> **//** *Ultimately, choking off North Korea's trade will depend upon participation of its two traditional allies and major trading partners—China and Russia.* **//**

Meanwhile, the chief of Seishin, another Japanese company, was arrested along with four employees in June [2003] over the export of grinding machines called jet mills to Iran in 1999–2000. The company is also suspected of selling a jet mill to Pyongyang in the mid-1990s, according to the Japanese media, and police are investigating to determine whether any more recent sales were made to the North. Jet mills crush solid objects with highly pressurized air, and are most commonly used to pulverize plastics and pharmaceuticals. They can, however, also boost missile thrust by turning solid rocket fuel into fine particles, and are a restricted export under Japanese law.

Those who have witnessed North Korean arms-manufacturing operations are not surprised that Japan is a source of components. Kim Do Sung, who defected from the North in 1997 and now goes by a pseudonym to protect relatives back home, says he worked for nine years at Plant 38, a huge armaments factory in the city of Huichon in the northern province of Jaggang [North Korea]. Kim says the vast majority of the computer chips and electronic components used in missile guidance systems there were Japanese. He recalls unloading a shipment of equipment from Japan that was like a Christmas stocking for missile scientists, packed with oscilloscopes for analyzing trajectory, special welding machines to make the seamless joints needed in a missile body, computer chips and picture tubes used in monitors to track missile routes. "Without foreign parts we couldn't have made the missiles," says Kim. "That's the main reason North Korea needs dollars."

Japan isn't the only shopping mall for North Korea's military machine. Pyongyang gets precursor chemicals for its chemical and biological weapons programs from Europe, China and Russia, according to U.S. and South Korean officials. The freighter that took the North Korean Scuds to Yemen returned to the North via Germany, loading up with a shipment of sodium cyanide—a chemical used in metal plating and gold extraction that can also be used to make nerve gas. That shipment was blocked by German and French authorities. Germany also . . . blocked a North Korea–bound consignment of aluminum tubes—key components for the centrifuges used to enrich uranium to bomb-grade quality. Chinese companies have sold specialty steel to North Korea for use in its missile program, as well as gyroscopes and accelerometers (used to measure vibration and g-force) that are potential missile parts. And Russian companies are suspected of selling high-strength maraging steel—used in missiles and centrifuge systems—to Pyongyang.

> *Underlying any action against the North is the risk that the rogue nation will do something crazy in response.*

The trade is hard to stop because it's impossible to tell whether so-called "dual-use" material and equipment are destined for peaceful purposes. North Korea is skilled at using front companies with ever-changing names to disguise the real end user. As a Western diplomat notes, a machine for freeze-drying coffee can also be used to make anthrax spores. Says Akio Igarashi of the Tokyo-based watchdog Center for Information on Security Trade Control: "With North Korea you don't know if a lunch box you export will end up as a container for nuclear material."

Tokyo is trying nonetheless to enhance screening of exports to the North. Ferry runs between the two countries by the Mangyongbong-92, a North Korean ship suspected of transporting spies and drugs into Japan and weapons parts out, were suspended by Pyongyang in June [2003] after Tokyo deployed an army of inspectors to Niigata dockyards to scour the vessel.

Japan has also blacklisted all trade with Pyongyang's Central Zoo, which is suspected of being a military front that uses its amusement-park rides as an excuse to procure electrical parts for missiles and other arms.

Ultimately, choking off North Korea's trade will depend upon participation of its two traditional allies and major trading partners—China and Russia. Senior U.S. officials, according to sources, are constantly wheedling China to deny overflight rights to suspicious planes exiting North Korea, without success. [On July 2003], China and Russia blocked a proposed condemnation of North Korea's nuclear arms program by the U.N. Security Council.

Underlying any action against the North is the risk that the rogue nation will do something crazy in response. Trying to stop ships and planes carrying hardware that represents one of the country's few sources of income could have "dangerous consequences," says Bermudez, the Jane's analyst. "What happens if the North Koreans open fire?"

Washington seems to calculate that the risk cannot be avoided without confronting far greater dangers later. Iran watcher Michael Ledeen of the American Enterprise Institute, citing sources in Iran, says a delegation of mullahs traveled to Pyongyang [in 2003] to discuss swapping nuclear technology for cash. It isn't known if the deal was concluded. But after the trip, top leaders of Iran's Revolutionary Guards were told that Iran would have its own nuclear weapons "soon," says Ledeen. Saddam Hussein's Iraq had no nukes. That regime is gone, but how much more frightening will Bush's "axis of evil" be a year from now?

4

North Korea's Military Policies Are Irrational

Ralph de Toledano

Ralph de Toledano is a Washington, D.C., columnist and a frequent writer for Insight on the News.

There is no rational explanation for President Kim Jong Il's devastating policies in North Korea. Given North Korea's weaknesses and size, it will never be able to dominate Asia or seriously threaten the United States. Kim Jong Il could use his power to prosper North Korea and win the gratitude of his people. Instead, he spends all his energies on developing a massive military and nuclear power that, if it is ever used, will destroy the country.

During the Cold War, there was some rationality to the actions of the Soviet Union. [Dictator] Josef Stalin and his successors had a vision shared with Napoleon and Genghis Khan of world hegemony. He could wrap this vision in a propaganda of social and economic revolution, but no one took this seriously, not even Stalin himself. [Former Iraqi dictator] Saddam Hussein could be thought to make some sense. He saw himself as another Saladin[1] who would lead an Arab empire and triumph over the West, as once before Islam had advanced on the Christian world, but lost out at Tours and Vienna.

But what could motivate North Korea's [leader] Kim Jong Il? Does he dream of Asian and eventually global hegemony? Even his wildest successes can make his country no more than a

1. a Muslim warrior and hero who in the twelfth century fought and defeated the Christian Crusaders who were trying to regain control of the Holy Land in the Middle East

Ralph de Toledano, "No Method Evident to Kim Jong Il's Madness," *Insight on the News*, June, 24, 2003. Copyright © 2004 by News World Communications, Inc. All rights reserved. Reproduced by permission.

thorn in the side of East and West, a nation-size suicide bomber. North Korea might have prospered, as South Korea has, and for this he would have had the gratitude of his people. But that is not the way history will mark him. Consider his record.

Kim Jong Il's record

The *Economist* reports that "for some time now, North Korea's economy has been close to a meltdown." Starvation and misery face everyone except the military and the political elite. The North Korean won has fallen from 2.15 to the dollar to 1.50 to the dollar, with the black market rate at 800. "The shelves of state-run shops are virtually empty," the *Economist* continues. "Hardly any factory in the country can turn a profit." Energy and fuel shortages have destroyed the economic viability of the country. Most hospitals are unable to provide adequate medical services or serious surgical treatment. Wages have fallen catastrophically below prices. China supplies 70 percent of the oil for what industry North Korea still has and gears its armed forces. Chinese food aid prevents total starvation. And, as observers are beginning to report, central authority exists unchallenged only in Pyongyang [capital of North Korea], with the countryside increasingly sliding into apathetic opposition.

> *Even [Kim Jong Il's] wildest successes can make his country no more than a thorn in the side of East and West, a nation-size suicide bomber.*

Given this situation, North Korea would be unable to fight a war of any duration. A military force needs a solid industrial base, and North Korea's is a shambles. Weapons of mass destruction can strike terror, but they cannot capture and occupy territory. True, North Korea could strike devastatingly at Seoul, the South Korean capital, which lies in easy missile range. But other than that, weapons of mass destruction would serve little military purpose and cut off delivery of solid food and essential oil from a China which is at best ambivalent.

President Kim can bring tragedy to his neighbors, but to what avail? He would invite the deadly counterblows of the United States, embarrass and antagonize China and bring on himself the outrage of the world. He and his Communist government believe that by lies, blackmail and missile-rattling they can make a slave out of the United States and frighten it into rehabilitating their economy on their terms and at no political cost.

Once upon a time, there might have been ideological considerations. But China and North Korea long since have rejected Marxism-Leninism as a political and economic nonstarter. They no longer believe that *Das Kapital*,[2] as full of theoretical holes as a slice of moldy Swiss cheese, is a viable economic blueprint. What remains is a totalitarian brutality and a philosophy embodying a passionate hate of all moral and human precepts, an amalgam of neo-Marxism and neo-Freudianism.

> *President Kim can bring tragedy to his neighbors, but to what avail?*

The country ground to a halt recently when China briefly cut off oil supplies. So Kim has said he would consider economic sanctions, which would bring his country to its knees, an act of war. He can take a few more potshots at U.S. planes. And of course he can complain to the United Nations, where he might have some support from France. Beyond this, he can convert North Korea into a nuclear suicide bomber. But being neither a fanatic like his father nor an idiot, Kim must know that this would be the end of his country.

What remains a mystery about North Korea, and about other rogue states, is a tremendous "why?" What does Kim get out of persecuting his people, starving them and destroying the economy? What does he get by threatening the world with weapons of mass destruction which have been created with the blood of his suffering people? He is all-powerful, but that power could have been directed toward making North Korea prosperous and strong.

All Kim reaps is hatred and fear, hardly something to make you sleep well at night. Ozymandias, in [Percy Bysshe] Shelley's poem, could boast that he was king of kings and say, "Look

---

2. An 1867 economic treatise by Karl Marx describing what he considered the injustices of capitalism.

upon my works, ye mighty, and despair." But Kim can point only to a bankrupt and miserable country, to an armory of lethal weapons and to a role as a national suicide bomber. Is that sufficient fulfillment? And he is not the only one. Perhaps [Cuba's dictator] Fidel Castro preens before the mirror, strokes his beard and giggles at the minor problems he has brought to the gringos. He and Kim will spend their allotted time on this planet, ending up honored and sung only in bitter measures.

5

North Korea Seeks to Force Reunification with South Korea

Homer T. Hodge

Homer T. Hodge is an associate with Booz Allen Hamilton, Inc., in McLean, Virginia. He is a former senior intelligence officer for Asia at the U.S. Army National Ground Intelligence Center (NGIC). Hodge is also a retired army officer and former Northeast Asia foreign area officer with service in Korea and Japan. His government service includes assignments with the National Security Agency and the Office of Special Advisor to the Commander, Combined Forces Command, in Korea.

North Korea's foremost national goal has historically been the reunification of the Korean Peninsula on North Korean terms. In fact, the country's constitution describes reunification with South Korea as "the supreme national task," and reunification continues to be a pervasive theme in the North Korean media. North Korea plans to achieve this goal of reunification through a military takeover of South Korea. It therefore allocates most of the country's scarce resources to the military, develops long-range ballistic missiles, and seeks nuclear weapons capability. The North Korean army, the fifth largest military force in the world, has positioned the majority of its ground forces to allow easy access into South Korea. Given North Korea's desperate economic problems, North Korean leaders see reunification on the North's terms as essential to the survival of the North Korean regime.

S imply put, military strategies derive from national strategies intended to achieve goals and conditions that satisfy national interests. Military strategies reflect capabilities vis a vis potential opponents, resource constraints, and desired end states. North Korea is no different; its military strategy is a reflection of [its] national goals. . . .

Pyongyang's foremost national goal

Historically, [the capital of North Korea] Pyongyang's foremost goal has been the reunification of the Korean peninsula on North Korean terms. The regime's constitution describes reunification as "the supreme national task," and it remains a consistently pervasive theme in North Korean media. However, despite what the North Koreans have continued to tell us for the past five decades, outside observers and specialists differ greatly over exactly what North Korea's goals really are.

Since at least the mid-1990s, there has been a widespread view among Korea observers that, because of severe economic decline, food shortages, and related problems, regime survival has replaced reunification as Pyongyang's most pressing objective. Further, these observers argue, despite its rhetoric, North Korea realizes that reunification through conquest of South Korea is no longer possible. There are also some who argue that the North Korean leadership has recognized the need to initiate substantial change in order to survive in the international community and is embarking on economic reform, reconciliation with South Korea, and reduction of military tensions. In addition to the goals of regime survival, reform, and reconciliation, there is another explanatory view of North Korea's foremost national goal that has been held by a minority of observers for several decades (and has been a consistent theme of North Korean media)—defense against foreign invasion by "imperialist aggressors and their lackey running dogs" [as the newspaper *Nodong Sinmun* has described it]. Adherents of this view believe that the North Korean leadership genuinely fears an attack by the United States and South Korea and maintains a strong military purely for defense. President Bush's reference to the "axis of evil" in his January 2002 State of the Union address, announcement of plans to adopt a "pre-emptive" military strategy, and increasing numbers of statements by Administration officials about US intentions to employ military force to remove Iraq's Saddam Hussein from power have added support to the

"defense" explanation. Some have also argued that enhance-
ment of the military by [President] Kim Jong Il serves primarily
to strengthen his domestic political power base. While there is
an obvious element of truth in this proposition, it is an over-
simplification that distorts the true role of military strength in
the regime.

Others accept North Korea's word that reunification remains the primary goal and argue that Pyongyang's long-term
strategy to dominate the peninsula by any means has not
changed. They cite North Korea's continued focus of scarce resources to the military, development of longer-range ballistic
missiles, and the recent revelation by Pyongyang that it seeks a
nuclear weapons capability as indications that reunification remains the foremost goal.

The evidence supports a reunification goal

The preponderance of evidence clearly supports the conclusion
that reunification under the leadership of Kim Jong Il, by whatever means, remains "the supreme national task." North Korean media rhetoric continues to extol reunification under
Kim. A parallel but closely related theme is that of completing
the socialist revolution. When North Korean leaders speak of
achieving "socialist revolution in our country," they mean unification of the entire peninsula on their terms. The Kim regime
in North Korea considers the entire peninsula as constituting
its sovereign territory. It does not recognize South Korea as being a separate nation, nor the government of South Korea as legitimate. Therefore, when North Korea refers to "our country"
or the "fatherland," they mean the entire Korean peninsula.
When read in the original Korean, the meaning of these terms
becomes much clearer. The North Korean leaders view the
southern half of their country as occupied by "US imperialists"
and the government of South Korea as "puppets serving their
imperialist masters." "Defense" does not refer to defending
North Korea, but to defending all of Korea. Accordingly, "defense of the fatherland" means (1) reclaiming that portion of
Korea—i.e., South Korea—that is currently occupied and controlled by the "imperialists," and (2) defending against further
encroachment by "US imperialists." While they certainly see
that the possibility of a popular armed revolution in South Korea, particularly one sympathetic to Pyongyang, is extremely
remote, reunification through force of arms appears to remain

possible to the North Korean leadership.

Without question, survival is a basic goal of incumbent regimes of all nation-states; North Korea is no exception. However, in the long term, reunification is essential to regime survival. In the near- to mid-term, North Korea may be able to "muddle through," economically, based on donations from the outside, primarily from the United States and South Korea.

However, pursuit of such a course can only lead to dependency and loss of control. Such dependency is inconsistent with the ideological tenet of Juche (self-reliance). The alternative to control of the entire peninsula is increasing dependence on South Korea, leading to complete economic absorption by Seoul and a breakdown of isolation and information control. The result would be the awakening of the North Korean populace to the true economic and social conditions of daily life in South Korea and, ultimately, the demise of the Kim regime. Clearly, regime survival, national defense, and a self-sufficient economy are logical goals; however, reunification of the peninsula remains the foremost goal that drives North Korea's national strategy.

In the North, the fear of conquest and defeat through economic absorption by South Korea undoubtedly has outweighed any fear of attack. North Korean leaders must know that time is on Seoul's side; if the South Koreans bide their time, the cost of slowly but steadily making inroads into North Korea through economic means is obviously far smaller than the price in terms of blood and treasure required to conquer the North militarily and then rebuild. South Korea enjoys an increasing and irreversible economic lead over North Korea.

A stronger case, based on recent events and statements of US officials, could be made to support the argument that North Korean leaders increasingly fear a US-led attack. The danger here is that as the North Korean leadership sees US actions in the war on terror, they may conclude that the United States intends to launch an attack to remove Kim Jong Il from power and decide to execute a preemptive surprise attack on South Korea. US initiation of military action against Iraq could prove to be the catalyst for a North Korean decision to go to war. While such an attack would be a gamble, the North Korean leadership could judge that the US focus on and concentration of military power in operations against Iraq would strengthen North Korea's chances of success.

North Korea's surprising admission to US Assistant Secretary of State James A. Kelly during talks in Pyongyang on 16 October 2002 that it has a secret ongoing nuclear weapons development program was probably prompted by increasing North Korean concerns about possible US military action.

Historical background

Knowledge of the 20th-century history of Korea is essential to understanding North Korean national interests and goals. Until the end of World War II in 1945, Korea had remained a single, ethnically and culturally homogenous country for over a thousand years. Initially divided on a temporary basis by the United States and Soviet Union along the 38th parallel to facilitate the surrender and demobilization of Japanese forces stationed in Korea, this division quickly became permanent as US-Soviet relations cooled. By 1948, two governments, each claiming sovereignty over the entire peninsula, had been established: the Soviet-supported communist Democratic People's Republic of Korea in the north, and the US-backed Republic of Korea in the south. The national policies of both Koreas have been shaped by the underlying aim of eventual reunification.

The all-encompassing impact on North Korea of the character, personality, life experiences, and thinking of its founder and first leader, Kim Il Sung, is probably unique among modern nations. The past and current history, nature, and direction of the country cannot be understood apart from Kim Il Sung; eight years after his death, his influence remains dominant. Kim's perspective on the world and his view of the purpose of political power and the state were defined by his early education in Chinese schools and ideological training by Chinese Communists, his experience as a guerrilla fighter with the Chinese Communists against the Japanese in Manchuria, and his military training and further political education in the Soviet Union during World War II. The wartime Soviet state became the model on which the North Korean regime was created by Kim Il Sung.

As a key element of his ideological models (Stalin, Mao),[1] "militarism" had a defining impact on Kim's thinking in his early formative years. The experience of the Korean War further strengthened this view. Kim, reflecting Maoist strategic

1. Joseph Stalin was the leader of the Communist Soviet Union until his death in 1953. Chairman Mao Zedong was the leader of Communist China until his death in 1976.

thought, saw contradictory elements as driving history. Conflict did not require a solution; it was the solution to political problems. Hence, politics and international relations were processes by which contradictions were resolved through conflict, and the nature of that conflict was zero-sum. Accordingly, to Kim, the purpose of the state, like the anti-Japanese guerrilla unit, was to wage war effectively. In his view, economic activity produced the means to wage war, education produced soldiers to wage war, and ideology convinced the people of the sociological and historical inevitability of war. For Kim, war in the near-term meant reunifying the Korean peninsula on Pyongyang's terms and, in the long-term, continuing the global struggle against US imperialism.

From this thinking and Kim's early experiences evolved a unique North Korean nationalism that was not so much inspired by Korean history or past cultural achievements as by the Spartan outlook of the anti-Japanese guerrillas. This nationalism focused on imagined past wrongs and promises of retribution for "national leaders" (i.e., South Korean officials) and their foreign backers (i.e., the United States). The nationalism of Kim Il Sung capitalized on historic xenophobia, stressing the "purity" of all things Korean against the "contamination" of foreign ideas, and inculcating the population with a sense of fear and animosity toward the outside world. Most important, this nationalism emphasized "that the guerrilla ethos was not only supreme, but also the only legitimate basis on which to reconstitute a reunified Korea" [according to scholar Adrian Buzo].

Militarism has remained an essential aspect of the character of the North Korean state since its founding in 1948; it constitutes a key element of the strategic culture of the regime. Accordingly, the maintenance of a powerful, offensive military force has always been and remains fundamental to the regime. This perspective was inculcated into the thinking of Kim's son and heir apparent, Kim Jong Il, throughout his life and is reflected in the younger Kim's policies, writings, and speeches. This militarism was the primary instrument to which he turned in order to deal with North Korea's severe economic crisis of the 1990s. Kim adopted the "military-first political method" as the means to survive and overcome this crisis. Accordingly, "military-first politics" is the key element in the current theme of creating a "strong and prosperous nation" that is capable of realizing completion of the "socialist revolution"— i.e., reunification. "Military-first politics" is more than the employment of military terminology to describe organization, discipline, and perseverance in accomplishment of public tasks; it emphasizes the need for a strong military even at the sacrifice of daily public needs. The abolition of the post of state President and simultaneous elevation of the position of Chairman, National Defense Commission, to the "highest post of state" in 1998 further underscores Kim's ideological commitment to militarism as the fundamental basis for regime survival. North Korea's military strategy, as a component of national strategy, reflects this commitment.

Pyongyang's military strategy

North Korea's military strategy is offensive and is designed to provide a military option to achieve reunification by force employing surprise, overwhelming firepower, and speed. It is shaped by the regime's militarist ideology and the strong influence of Soviet and Russian military thinking with historical roots in the Korean nationalist resistance against Japanese colonialism, the Korean experience in the Chinese Civil War, and international events of the early Cold War years as interpreted by the late Kim Il Sung. Continued emphasis on maintaining this strategy, despite severe economic decline, suggests that Pyongyang continues to perceive an offensive military strategy as a viable option for ensuring regime survival and realizing reunification on North Korean terms.

The offensive character of Pyongyang's military strategy is demonstrated by the organization and deployment of its forces. The primary instrument of this strategy is North Korea's armed forces, known collectively as the Korean People's Army (KPA).

The KPA of 2003 is an imposing and formidable force of 1.17 million active personnel with a reserve force of over 5 million, making it the fifth largest military force in the world. The ground forces are organized into eight infantry corps, four mechanized corps, an armor corps, and two artillery corps. The KPA air force consists of 92,000 personnel, and is equipped with some 730 mostly older combat aircraft and 300 helicopters. The 46,000-man KPA navy is primarily a coastal force. Additionally, the KPA maintains the largest special operations force (SOF) in the world, consisting of approximately 100,000 highly trained, totally dedicated soldiers. A long history of bloody incursions into South Korea underscores the offensive mission of this force.

The overwhelming majority of active ground forces is deployed in three echelons—a forward operational echelon of four infantry corps; supported by a second operational echelon of two mechanized corps, the armor corps, and an artillery corps; and a strategic reserve of the two remaining mechanized corps and the other artillery corps. These forces are garrisoned along major north-south lines of communication that provide rapid, easy access to avenues of approach into South Korea. The KPA has positioned massive numbers of artillery pieces, especially its longer-range systems, close to the Demilitarized Zone (DMZ) that separates the two Koreas.

Soviet concepts of deep operations required the employment of air forces capable of achieving air superiority and air-deliverable ground forces; lacking the resources to produce or deploy such forces, the KPA compensated by greatly increasing deployment of conventional cannon and rocket artillery and tactical and strategic SOF.

> *Militarism has remained an essential aspect of the character of the North Korean state since its founding in 1948.*

Key elements of Pyongyang's military strategy include the employment of weapons of mass destruction, including nuclear (as recently revealed by Pyongyang), and missile systems including short- and medium-range and probably intercontinental missiles. The commander of US forces in Korea assesses that North Korea has large chemical weapon stockpiles, is self-sufficient in the production of chemical agents, and may have produced enough plutonium for at least two nuclear weapons. North Korea has now demonstrated the capability to strike targets throughout the entire territory of the Republic of Korea (ROK) and Japan, as well as large portions of China and Russia. In an attack on South Korea, Pyongyang could use its missiles in an attempt to isolate the peninsula from strategic reinforcement and intimidate or punish Japan. North Korea's inventory of ballistic missiles includes over 500 SCUD short-range ballistic missiles that can hit any target in South Korea and medium-range No Dong missiles capable of reaching Japan and the US bases there. While they have not flight-tested long-range missiles—at least, in North Korea—they have continued research, development, and rocket engine testing.

Although this is an offensive strategy, there are defensive aspects to it. An army must protect its flanks whether attacking or defending. This principle takes on added importance for a peninsular state such as Korea. Both geography and history have taught the North Koreans the vital necessity of protecting their coasts; during the Korean War, United Nations forces conducted two major amphibious operations in Korea, one on each coast. The KPA continues to improve coastal defenses, especially in the forward area. They have established or strengthened air defense positions around airfields, near major ports, and along the primary highway between Pyongyang and the DMZ. Additionally, there is a corps-size capital defense command responsible for the defense of Pyongyang. However, KPA force deployment lacks defensive depth at the operational level of war. The North Koreans have not constructed defensive belts across the peninsula similar to Forward Edge of the Battle Area (FEBA) Alfa, Bravo, and Charlie in South Korea. While there are local defensive positions along lines of communication and key intersections manned by local militia and reserve units, they have not established an operational-level network of defensive strong points interlocked with obstacles and planned defensive fires. The forward-deployed artillery is sufficiently close to the DMZ that, in a defensive role, it would be vulnerable to surprise and early destruction by attack from South Korea.

Taken together, these facts strengthen the judgment that Pyongyang's military strategy is not defensive but offensive. A strong argument can probably also be made that North Korean military strategy would remain offensive even if defense against a feared attack replaced reunification as the foremost goal of the regime. North Korea's "militarist" culture advocates offense as the most effective means of defense. . . .

North Korea will not abandon its offensive military policy

The ideological underpinnings and strategic culture of North Korea's regime emphasize the dominance of militarism epitomized by a strong army. Reunification of the peninsula on North Korean terms remains the foremost strategic goal of the regime. North Korea's severe and probably irreversible economic decline over the past decade places the regime's survival in question. Therefore, North Korean leaders must see reunification on their terms not only as their historic purpose but also as essential to long-term survival. Continued investment in a powerful military organized and deployed to execute an offensive military strategy, despite its drain on a moribund economy, strongly suggests that North Korean leaders perceive its military as probably the only remaining instrument for realization of that goal. At the same time, they must realize that time is not on their side.

In his book, *The Origins of Major War*, Dale Copeland sets forth a strong argument that a state facing irreversible economic decline but still possessing military power vis-a-vis a competing state may resort to preventive war, especially if it perceives its own decline as deep and inevitable. One might counter by arguing that Pyongyang must know that it lacks any military superiority over the United States, which guarantees the defense of South Korea through the security treaty. This is no doubt true, as evidenced by the effective deterrence of a US military presence in South Korea for the past five decades. However, it is not so certain that Kim Jong Il judges South Korean military forces alone as superior to the KPA. North Korea's continued insistence that the question of reunification can be settled only among Koreans, and that the withdrawal of all foreign forces is essential to that process, suggests that Pyongyang would prefer to deal militarily with the South Korean army alone.

North Korea's military strategy remains an offensive strategy designed to achieve reunification by force. While the KPA has deployed forces to protect its coasts, airfields, and especially the North Korean capital of Pyongyang, the overall forward deployment of forces and, particularly, forward deployment of large numbers of long-range artillery underscore the offensive nature of its strategy.

Renunciation of reunification as its premier goal, shifting to a defensive military strategy, or dismantling of the military force to achieve it would gravely undermine the raison d'etre of the regime. North Korean leaders see the demise of the Soviet Union as primarily the result of [former president Mikhail] Gorbachev's "New Thinking," which included the shift of the Soviet Union's military strategy to "defensive defense." Therefore, regime survival depends on staying the course. Simply stated, Pyongyang cannot abandon its offensive military strategy.

6

North Korea Must Transform Its Policies to Survive

John Bolton

John Bolton is the U.S. undersecretary of state for arms control and international security.

The North Korean government has created a tragedy, preventing economic development and starving its people while at the same time funding a massive military force armed with missiles and weapons of mass destruction (WMD). North Korea has an active chemical weapons program capable of producing and delivering various chemical agents as well as one of the most robust offensive biological weapons programs on earth. In addition, U.S. intelligence suggests that North Korea has produced enough plutonium for at least one, and possibly two, nuclear weapons and continues its efforts to acquire technology that could be used in its nuclear program. Finally, in addition to its WMD activities, North Korea is the world's main seller of ballistic missiles and related technology, which could be used to deliver WMD to military targets. The United States is demanding that North Korea stop its development of weapons of mass destruction and its exporting of missiles. Without these changes, North Korea may not survive.

The Republic of Korea [formal name of South Korea] has blossomed as a democracy, as a cutting edge high-tech economy, and as an example of impressive social change, not only for Asia but in many ways for the world. In sharp contrast

John Bolton, speech, Seoul, North Korea, August 29, 2002.

49

. . . North Korea is a self-created and self-perpetuated tragedy. For decades Pyongyang [the capital of North Korea] has strangled its own economic development and starved its people while building a massive military force armed with missiles and weapons of mass destruction. Without sweeping restructuring to transform itself and its relations with the world, the North's survival is in doubt.

Changes necessary for North Korea

Recently, we have seen hopeful signs of potential change. The revival of North-South dialog and the beginning of discussions with Japan on steps that could lead toward normalization have captured headlines. Perhaps even more importantly the DPRK [Democratic People's Republic of Korea, the formal name for North Korea] has begun to implement some initial steps at freeing prices and allowing private markets to exist. Whether all this flows from their desperation or their inspiration still is an open question. However, if such reforms continue and expand, the future of the North Korean people could be much brighter. As Secretary [of State Colin] Powell has said, "The past does not have to be the future for Pyongyang and its people. We believe that the light of transformation can start to shine where darkness currently prevails. To move this process forward we believe the North should quickly live up to its standing agreements with the South—for example, extending a rail link to the South, establishing free trade zones at Kaesong [a city in North Korea] and elsewhere, as well as reuniting separated family members." President Bush has repeatedly emphasized that we support dialog between the North and the South. He has also made clear that our deepest sympathies lie with the oppressed and starving North Korean people, for whom we have provided the largest amount of humanitarian assistance, this year [2002] including 155,000 metric tons of grain.

The North must also begin implementing military confidence building and tension reduction measures. Some 30 kilometers from where I stand lies one of the most dangerous places on Earth—the demilitarized zone [the dividing line between North and South Korea]. The 38th Parallel serves as a dividing line between freedom and oppression, between right and wrong. The brave forces of our two countries stand ready to defend against an evil regime that is armed to the teeth, including with weapons of mass destruction and ballistic missiles. It is a regime that has just a few miles from Seoul [the capital of South Korea] the most massive concentration of tubed artillery and rocketry on earth. We in America must always be cognizant of this enormous conventional threat to the South and especially to the people of [its] thriving capital.

Change in the North's diplomatic, economic, and security posture is necessary, but not sufficient, for it to join the community of nations. Today, perhaps our gravest concern is Pyongyang's continuing development of weapons of mass destruction and exporting the means to deliver them. I must say personally that this administration has repeatedly put the North on notice that it must get out of the business of proliferation. Nonetheless, we see few, if any, signs of change on this front. Too frequently North Korea acts as if the world will keep looking the other way. Unfortunately, the global consequences of its proliferation activities are impossible to ignore.

North Korea's chemical and biological weapons

Since I am Secretary Powell's senior advisor on Arms Control and International Security, let me provide a panoramic view of North Korea's WMD activities—chemical, biological, and nuclear as well as the export of missiles and missile technology—and thus explain to you here in South Korea why we are so concerned and the nature of the challenge I believe we face together.

In regard to chemical weapons, there is little doubt that North Korea has an active program. This adds to the threat to the people of Seoul and to the Republic of Korea (ROK)-US frontline troops. Despite our efforts to get North Korea to become a party to the Chemical Weapons Convention, they have refused to do so. Indeed, dating back to 1961, when Kim Il-sung [then president of North Korea] issued a public 'Declaration of Chemicalization,' North Korea has flouted international norms. Both of our governments recognize this threat. In a recent report to Congress, the US government declared that North Korea "is capable of producing and delivering via missile warheads or other munitions a wide variety of chemical agents." A recent Defense White Paper published by the South Korean government concurred, noting that North Korea has a minimum of 2,500 tons of lethal chemicals, and that North Korea is "exerting its utmost efforts to produce chemical weapons."

The news on the biological weapons front is equally disturbing. The governments of both the United States and South

Korea are aware that the North possesses an active bioweapons program. Indeed, at times the North has flaunted it. In the 1980s, the North Korean military intensified this effort as instructed by then-President Kim Il-sung, who declared that "poisonous gas and bacteria can be used effectively in war."

> *// For decades, Pyongyang has strangled its own economic development and starved its people while building a massive military force armed with missiles and weapons of mass destruction. //*

Both North and South Korea became signatories to the Biological Weapons Convention in 1987, but only the South has lived up to its commitments under this treaty. [South Korea also] made a historic decision to go further and withdraw from the reservation clause in the Geneva Protocol and wholly prohibit the use of biological weapons.

But what can be said of North Korea? The US government believes that North Korea has one of the most robust offensive bioweapons programs on earth. North Korea to date is in stark violation of the Biological Weapons [BW] Convention. The United States believes North Korea has a dedicated, national-level effort to achieve a BW capability and that it has developed and produced, and may have weaponized, BW agents in violation of the Convention. North Korea likely has the capability to produce sufficient quantities of biological agents within weeks of a decision to do so.

The North's nuclear weapons program

Let's turn our attention now to the nuclear question. The US has had serious concerns about North Korea's nuclear weapons program for many years. In a recent report to Congress, the US Intelligence Community stated that "North Korea has produced enough plutonium for at least one, and possibly two nuclear weapons." Moreover, "Pyongyang continued its attempts to procure technology worldwide that could have application in its nuclear program."

It is true that North Korea has frozen plutonium production activities at the Yongbyon facility as required by the

Agreed Framework of 1994 and has allowed a large number of spent fuel rods that could otherwise be used to make nuclear weapons to be stored safely under international supervision. Still these important steps are only part of the agreement. Outstanding concerns remain. To signal our concerns about these unresolved questions, President Bush, for the first time since the signing of the Agreement in 1994, this year [2002] did not certify to the US Congress that North Korea is in compliance with all provisions.

The fact is that North Korea has not begun to allow inspectors with the International Atomic Energy Agency [IAEA] to complete all of their required tasks. Many doubt that North Korea ever intends to fully comply with its NPT [Nuclear Nonproliferation Treaty] obligations. Whatever one thinks, the bottom line is that [the] North has delayed for years bringing the required safeguards agreement into force.

> *The US has had serious concerns about North Korea's nuclear weapons program for many years.*

Pyongyang's record of the past 8 years does not inspire confidence. It has gone so far as to demand compensation for lost power generation, when its self-constructed barriers are largely to blame for construction delays. If the North has nothing to hide, then full cooperation with the IAEA, as required by its Safeguards Agreement and under the Agreed Framework, should be an easy task. Opening up to IAEA inspectors is the best way to remove suspicions and ensure the delivery of the light water reactors in a timely fashion.

The math is simple. Earlier this month [August 2002], concrete was poured at Kumho, the facility where the light water reactors [LWRs] are to be built. Construction of a significant portion of the first LWR is now scheduled to be complete by May 2005, at which time the construction schedule calls for delivery of controlled nuclear components. The problem is that key nuclear components to power the reactors cannot and will not be delivered until the IAEA effectively accounts for North Korea's nuclear activities—past and perhaps present. The IAEA estimates that these inspections will take at least three to four years with full cooperation from North Korea. It is now late summer 2002. Every day that the North fails to allow unfettered IAEA inspections necessarily pushes back the possible completion of the light water reactors.

Continued intransigence on the part of Pyongyang only begs the question: What is North Korea hiding? The concerns of the international community are only deepened by the clear discrepancy between the amount of plutonium that may have been reprocessed at the Yongbyon facility and the amount Pyongyang declared to the IAEA in 1992. The IAEA declared the North's explanations inadequate. As you recall, when the IAEA wanted to inspect waste sites in North Korea in 1992 to help construct the history of the North's nuclear program, the sites were deemed off-limits. If the North's IAEA declarations were accurate, then why not allow verification to occur?

The North could easily answer this question if it complied with the IAEA inspections required under the NPT. In a notable step backward just this past June [2002], however, North Korea withdrew its agreement to discuss the Verification of Completeness and Correctness of the initial declaration of plutonium with the IAEA. This must be changed. If the North is serious and not just using delaying tactics, then it must let the IAEA do its job.

North Korea needs to fulfill its pledge to Seoul when it committed itself to a nuclear free peninsula by signing the Joint North-South Denuclearization Agreement of 1992. That accord mandated random reciprocal inspections and committed both North and South to a nuclear-free peninsula. The South has lived up to its end of the bargain and the North has been handed a real opportunity to improve the welfare of its people and stability on the Peninsula. If the North is serious about peace and reconciliation, then it will do the same.

North Korea's global missile threat

In addition to its disturbing WMD activities, North Korea also is the world's foremost peddler of ballistic missile-related equipment, components, materials, and technical expertise. As the CIA [U.S. Central Intelligence Agency] publicly reports: "North Korea has assumed the role as the missile and manufacturing technology source for many programs. North Korean willingness to sell complete systems and components has enabled other states to acquire longer range capabilities." It has an impressive list of customers spanning the globe from the Middle East, South Asia to North Africa, with notable rogue-state clients such as Syria, Libya and Iran.

President Bush's use of the term "axis of evil" to describe Iran, Iraq, and North Korea was more than a rhetorical flourish—it was factually correct. First, the characteristics of the three countries' leadership are much the same: the leaders feel only they are important, not the people. Indeed, in North Korea, the people can starve as long as the leadership is well fed. Second, there is a hard connection between these regimes—an "axis"—along which flow dangerous weapons and dangerous technology.

> *In addition to its disturbing WMD activities, North Korea also is the world's foremost peddler of ballistic missile-related equipment, components, materials, and technical expertise.*

Let us use the case of Iran. For some years now, North Korea has provided Iran—arguably the most egregious state sponsor of terror—with medium-range ballistic missiles known as No Dongs. Iran has used this assistance and technology to strengthen its Shahab-3 program. The proliferation relationship may work in reverse, and the fruits of this cooperation could be offered for sale on the international market. Exports of ballistic missiles and related technology are one of the North's major sources of hard currency, which fuel continued missile development and production.

North Korea must choose transformation

North Korea today faces a choice. If North Korea wants to have a brighter future, it needs to fundamentally shift the way it operates at home and abroad. After all, the Soviet Union had 30,000 nuclear warheads and in the end it still collapsed due to its own contradictions.

Working in lockstep with our allies, South Korea and Japan, the United States is prepared to take big steps to help the North transform itself and move our relations toward normalcy. However, our actions in large part will be incumbent on the DPRK's positive movement across a number of fronts. Among other steps, we insist that the North get out of the missile proliferation business. As President Bush has said, "We cannot permit the world's most dangerous regimes to export the world's most dangerous weapons." Also, the North must open up to IAEA inspection and show that it is committed to a nuclear free peninsula. . . .

Last but certainly not least, simple decency demands that the North alleviate the suffering and malnutrition of its citizens. To help the people of North Korea, the US remains committed to the World Food Program's operations in the DPRK. With much better monitoring and access, we could do even more. But international charity alone can't save the North Korean people from tragedy. Economic and political transformation are vital.

During his visit in February [2002] to South Korea, President Bush made our intentions clear. He stipulated that we have no intention of invading North Korea. Rather, he said, "We're prepared to talk with the North about steps that would lead to a better future, a future that is more hopeful and less threatening." We continue to stand by this offer of dialogue—anytime, anyplace.

Today, however, as President Bush stressed, the stability of the [Korean] Peninsula is built on the successful and strong alliance between the ROK-US. No matter what the future holds, we will stand by the government and people of South Korea.

7

North Korea Must Protect Itself from Vicious U.S. Policies

The Democratic People's Republic of Korea

The Democratic People's Republic of Korea is the formal name for North Korea.

North Korea's sovereignty and security have been violated by vicious and hostile U.S. policies. The International Atomic Energy Agency (IAEA) is being used as a tool for implementing these policies. On January 6, 2003, the United States persuaded the IAEA to adopt a resolution that called North Korea a "criminal" and demanded it scrap its nuclear program and give up its right to self-defense. At the same time, the IAEA said nothing about U.S. violations of the Nuclear Non-Proliferation Treaty and the 1994 Agreed Framework. According to the Agreed Framework between North Korea and the United States, North Korea agreed to freeze its nuclear program in exchange for fuel oil and aid in building light water reactors for electrical production. However, the United States has stopped the supply of fuel oil to North Korea. In addition, the United States has listed North Korea as part of an "axis of evil" and targeted it for "pre-emptive nuclear attack." The United States has responded to North Korea's proposal for negotiations with threats of a blockade and military punishment. Only if the United States drops its hostile policy will North Korea provide evidence that it is not making nuclear weapons.

The Democratic People's Republic of Korea, Statement on NPT Withdrawal, January 10, 2003.

Editor's Note: In January 2003 North Korea announced that it was withdrawing from the Nuclear Non-proliferation Treaty, the main means by which the United States and other countries seek to control nuclear weapons proliferation. The following is North Korea's official announcement of this action.

A dangerous situation where our nation's sovereignty and our state's security are being seriously violated is prevailing on the Korean Peninsula due to the US vicious hostile policy towards the DPRK.[1]

The United States controls the IAEA

The United States instigated the International Atomic Energy Agency (IAEA) to adopt another "resolution" against the DPRK on 6 January [2003] in the wake of a similar "resolution" made on 29 November, 2002.

Under its manipulation, the IAEA in those "resolutions" termed the DPRK "a criminal" and demanded it scrap what the US called a "nuclear programme" at once by a verifiable way in disregard of the nature of the nuclear issue, a product of the US hostile policy towards the DPRK, and its unique status in which it declared suspension of the effectuation of its withdrawal from the Nuclear Non-Proliferation Treaty (NPT).

> *It is none other than the US which wrecks peace and security on the Korean Peninsula and drives the situation there to an extremely dangerous phase.*

Following the adoption of the latest "resolution", the IAEA director general issued an ultimatum that the agency would bring the matter to the UN Security Council to apply sanctions against the DPRK unless it implements the "resolution" in a few weeks.

This clearly proves that the IAEA still remains a servant and a spokesman for the US and the NPT is being used as a tool for implementing the US hostile policy towards the DPRK aimed

1. Democratic People's Republic of Korea, the formal name for North Korea

to disarm it and destroy its system by force.

A particular mention should be made of the fact that the IAEA in the recent "resolution" kept mum about the US which has grossly violated the NPT and the DPRK-US agreed framework, but urged the DPRK, the victim, to unconditionally accept the US demand for disarmament and forfeit its right to self-defence, and the agency was praised by the US for "saying all what the US wanted to do." This glaringly reveals the falsehood and hypocrisy of the signboard of impartiality the IAEA put up.

The DPRK government vehemently rejects and denounces this "resolution" of the IAEA, considering it as a grave encroachment upon our country's sovereignty and the dignity of the nation.

The United States is creating a crisis

It is none other than the US which wrecks peace and security on the Korean Peninsula and drives the situation there to an extremely dangerous phase.

After the appearance of the Bush administration, the United States listed the DPRK as part of an "axis of evil", adopting it as a national policy to oppose its system, and singled it out as a target of pre-emptive nuclear attack, openly declaring a nuclear war.

Systematically violating the DPRK-US Agreed Framework [AF], the US brought up another "nuclear suspicion" and stopped the supply of heavy oil, reducing the AF to a dead document. It also answered the DPRK's sincere proposal for the conclusion of the DPRK-US non-aggression treaty and its patient efforts for negotiations with such threats as "blockade" and "military punishment" and with such an arrogant attitude as blustering that it may talk but negotiations are impossible.

The US went so far to instigate the IAEA to internationalize its moves to stifle the DPRK, putting its declaration of a war into practice. This has eliminated the last possibility of solving the nuclear issue of the Korean Peninsula in a peaceful and fair way.

It was due to such nuclear war moves of the US against the DPRK and the partiality of the IAEA that the DPRK was compelled to declare its withdrawal from the NPT in March 1993 when a touch-and-go situation was created on the Korean Peninsula.

As it has become clear once again that the US persistently seeks to stifle the DPRK at any cost and the IAEA is used as a tool for executing the US hostile policy towards the DPRK, we can no longer remain bound to the NPT, allowing the country's security and the dignity of our nation to be infringed upon.

North Korea withdraws
from the NPT in self-defense

Under the grave situation where our state's supreme interests are most seriously threatened, the DPRK government adopts the following decisions to protect the sovereignty of the country and the nation and their right to existence and dignity: firstly, the DPRK government declares an automatic and immediate effectuation of its withdrawal from the NPT, on which "it unilaterally announced a moratorium as long as it deemed necessary" according to the 11 June, 1993, DPRK-US joint statement, now that the US has unilaterally abandoned its commitments to stop nuclear threat and renounce hostility towards the DPRK in line with the same statement.

Secondly, it declares that the DPRK withdrawing from the NPT is totally free from the binding force of the safeguards accord with the IAEA under its Article 3.

The withdrawal from the NPT is a legitimate self-defensive measure taken against the US moves to stifle the DPRK and the unreasonable behaviour of the IAEA following the US. Though we pull out of the NPT, we have no intention to produce nuclear weapons and our nuclear activities at this stage will be confined only to peaceful purposes such as the production of electricity.

If the US drops its hostile policy to stifle the DPRK and stops its nuclear threat to the DPRK, the DPRK may prove through a separate verification between the DPRK and the US that it does not make any nuclear weapon.

The United States and the IAEA will never evade their responsibilities for compelling the DPRK to withdraw from the NPT, by ignoring the DPRK's last efforts to seek a peaceful settlement of the nuclear issue through negotiations.

8

North Korea Must Be Disarmed

Hwang Jang Yop

Hwang Jang Yop was a high-ranking member of the North Korean government for forty years and a chief architect of the juche *(self-reliance) ideology of North Korea. He defected to South Korea in 1997 and now advocates efforts by South Korea, the United States, and other countries to remove the North Korean regime.*

Democratic countries must stop despotic regimes like North Korea from possessing weapons of mass destruction. Although some argue that it is dangerous to confront North Korean dictator Kim Jong Il because he might start a nuclear war, it is ridiculous to believe that North Korea would be capable of fighting a war against the United States with only a few atomic bombs. In fact, Kim Jong Il is a coward who only makes threats to gain economic aid. The United States must not agree to give North Korea any security guarantees or withdraw its forces in South Korea because Kim Jong Il would then attack South Korea and attempt to establish a pro–North Korean regime there. The United States, Japan, and South Korea must work together to disarm and reform North Korea.

Editor's Note: The following is a speech given on April 26, 2003, by Hwang Jang Yop at a convention in South Korea hosted by the Network for North Korean Human Rights and Democracy.

I would like to use this opportunity to comment on the North Korean nuclear problem, which is an issue that involves all

Hwang Jang Yop, speech before The Network for North Korean Human Rights and Democracy, South Korea, April 27, 2003.

of us striving to promote democracy in the North.

What is the fundamental principle that we should adhere to in our efforts to democratize North Korea? It is none other than the principle of democracy. This means that we have to unify the two Koreas based on democratic principles and by democratizing North Korea. Democracy should never become an object of compromise. It is the overriding principle.

The reason we so yearn for unification is because we want to preserve democracy and spread democratic values across the nation. Of course, both peace and unification are important goals. However, peace and unification that come at the expense of democracy are useless. Can we expect Kim Jong Il to spearhead unification? No way. Again, unification and peace must be based on democracy.

North Korea's possession of nuclear weapons is nothing new

North Korea's despotic leadership proclaimed that they have nuclear weapons. Actually, this is nothing new. Back in 1994—when I was in North Korea—the North Korean leadership was already discussing this matter, that they would confront the world by proclaiming possession of nukes. South Koreans and Americans were the ones unaware of this fact. But those already in the North Korean leadership knew about it. I also explained this situation when I came to South Korea.

What principle should we adhere to in resolving the North Korean nuclear crisis? The first and foremost principle is that democratic countries must arm themselves while having despotic regimes disarmed. A nuclear weapon is not evil in itself. If it were evil, then why would large countries possess them? Who says big countries can have nukes and small countries cannot? To say so is nonsense and very unfair. It may be more reasonable to say that small and weak countries are the ones who need those weapons the most so that they can protect themselves from pressure by powerful countries. . . .

Possession of weapons of mass destruction can be justified depending on whether the nature of the possessing country is democratic or despotic. Isn't it appropriate for a cop to arm oneself? But it is dangerous when criminals have weapons, which is why they need to be disarmed. Then what is the nature of the Kim Jong Il regime? It is a terrorist group and stands foremost in the so-called 'axis of evil.' If we were to compare

Kim Jong Il with [former Iraqi dictator] Saddam Hussein, I think Kim is the big brother and Hussein is the lastborn. What I mean is that Kim Jong Il is far more egregious than Hussein.

> *Since the North Korean regime is a criminal group, its possession of weapons of mass destruction must be severely dealt with.*

Since the North Korean regime is a criminal group, its possession of weapons of mass destruction must be severely dealt with. That it must be disarmed is our stance as a democratic state. Disapproval of North Korea's nuclear armament for the sake of preserving our democratic values. This is the number one principle.

The second principle is that we should not beg a despotic regime for peace just because we are afraid of its possession of nuclear weapons. We must fight against them in order to support and preserve the system of democracy. But opinions differ over this issue because some say we should fight against North Korea's dictatorship while others make the case that we should provide security guarantee and economic assistance. The reason people call for the latter is because they are fearful of the Kim Jong Il regime wielding nuclear weapons. These people say, "Isn't it better to provide security guarantee and assistance than to totally be wiped out by North Korea's nukes?" They are scared of the threats that the bad guys are posing.

North Korea is incapable of starting a nuclear war

North Koreans, including Kim Jong Il, talk about a nuclear war on the Korean Peninsula as if they have the capacity to fight such a war against the U.S. It is ridiculous. How can they fight such a war with only a handful of atomic bombs? They do have such bombs, by the way. They already completed manufacturing them when I was in North Korea. But how can North Korea use them when the U.S. might retaliate by showering its nuclear weapons on North Korea? It doesn't make sense for North Korea to fight a nuclear war against the U.S. Kim Jong Il is the most self-centered man on earth who does not have the courage to start a war.

You might think Kim Jong Il may still start a war if he is pushed to the wall. But no, that is not true. Kim Jong Il already has a huge amount of illicit funds piled up for himself. Moreover, he can always find a way to live because countries like China and Russia are willing to provide him with food. You have to understand that Kim Jong Il is an extremely selfish person. So selfish that he would not even blink an eye at the sight of millions of North Koreans starving to death so long as he can maintain his power. Why would a man like him dare to provoke war and risk his own life? It is nonsense. You need not worry about North Korea opening war. Everything coming out of Kim Jong Il's mouth is a mere threat. He doesn't have the courage to start a war nor does he feel the need to.

An airplane hijacker may need the courage to kill himself because of the nature of his mission. But why would Kim Jong Il feel the need to do so when an utmost status is already guaranteed for him? Moreover, he is well aware that the U.S., Korea and Japan are not willing to overthrow his regime by force. Therefore, his talk of using nuclear weapons is nothing but a threat. So there is nothing to be fearful of.

Concessions should not be granted to North Korea

Regime [change] is something for people of [North Korea] to decide. I mean, how can outsiders decide it for them? So North Korea asking for security guarantees only proves the servile spirit it has. Moreover, allowing North Korea to maintain its current regime is an act of supporting dictatorship and abandoning the North Korean people. Such isn't an act of democracy. It is crime and treason. Thus, it makes no sense to provide security assurance to the North. One who says security assurance is needed is not a supporter of democracy.

Kim Jong Il cannot aim beyond the goal of becoming the leader of a unified Korea. That's it. I mean, he wouldn't dare attempt to dominate Japan, China or the U.S., right? He is very scared of the U.S. He always says, "The U.S. is a scary country." Even his father, Kim Il Sung, told him to never open an attack against South Korea if U.S. forces are there. So Kim Jong Il triggering a nuclear war is nonsense. He is just trying to pose threats.

Then what does Kim Jong Il really want? Economic assistance is what he wants. I personally think it is highly likely that Kim Jong Il will eventually pretend like he is willing to give up nuclear armament, acting as if he is making a concession. He already has nuclear weapons kept under lock and key anyway, so how can anyone find them? He thinks that by doing so, his regime's security will be guaranteed. If Kim Jong Il says he will give up the nuclear program, the U.S. would probably congratulate itself for having pressured Kim into surrender. But this is the worst conclusion that can be reached.

> *We have to prevent North Korea's provocation by strengthening our alliance with the U.S. and Japan and by beefing up our military power.*

If we allow it to happen, Kim Jong Il will call for signing of a peace accord, citing 'security assurance' as the ostensible purpose. Actually, he is not even concerned about regime security. Then what would happen once a peace accord is signed? Kim Jong Il will call for withdrawal of the U.S. forces in South Korea. South Korea is swarming with pro-North Korean forces. When the two Koreas have a peace agreement, such forces will ask U.S. soldiers to leave the Peninsula (as they did during the candlelight vigils held in memory of the two Korean girls killed by a U.S. armored vehicle). If that happens, who knows? The U.S. might become hands-off to Korea issues.

Kim Jong Il seems to think that he can, based on North Korea's military strength, carry out a federation and establish a pro-North Korean regime in the South. That is why he is constantly asking for a security guarantee and a peace agreement. We should not allow ourselves to be deceived.

Concerning economic assistance, it is something that we should provide. Yes, we should help residents of North Korea by providing food and clothing. However, we should be very discerning in giving aid. What is happening to the aid that we provide? We found out that the rice provisions go first to the North Korean military. To earn foreign currency, Kim Jong Il orders the leftovers to be sold in markets. We must not allow this to happen. Assistance must be given in the context of weakening North Korea's dictatorship and strengthening democracy. That is why unconditional provision of assistance is undesirable.

Then what is our task at hand? It is to change North Korea's dictatorial regime into a democratic one. We must not allow

Secondly, we have to sever North Korea's links with China and Russia. These two countries continue to help the North and establish unjust relationships with it. Thus, we should first tell China that helping Kim Jong Il—for example, with defection issues—is becoming a stigma for China. That if China continues its support for the North, the international community may boycott Chinese products, refuse to participate in the upcoming Olympics, and that Japan and Taiwan may go nuclear.

Reform must be promoted in North Korea

Again, focusing on North Korea's human rights violations and severing its links with China and Russia are the preconditions for winning North Korea without fighting a war.

What next? Well, we should then induce reform within the North Korean society. I have met many Americans who suggest airing broadcasts to North Korea the way it was done to former socialist states of Europe. They also ask me what kind of broadcasts would be effective.

Well, I think it is premature to air such broadcasts toward the North. I had a chance to tour socialist countries of Europe during their collapse period. Those countries were heaven compared to North Korea. They had so much more freedom, that is. European states at least had democratic foundations from the past. That is why the most autocratic European countries like Rumania were unable to block broadcasts coming from foreign countries. But things are very different in North Korea. North Korea is a despotic and feudalistic country.

North Korea needs to be reformed to a certain extent. It most needs agricultural reform. Residents must be allowed to plant what they want and sell produce. It is unlikely for outside broadcasts to reach North Korean residents. The outside world must stop offering free aid to North Korea. Free aid from South Korea is what is making Kim Jong Il drag his feet on reform.

After inducing North Korea to reform, we have to then establish refugee camps for North Koreans in China and Russia. Doing so would require less than one-tenth of the money spent for opening the war in Iraq. Then, we should provide aid to these refugees.

If this happens, change will start from within North Korea. It is not because North Koreans do not have courage that they are not changing. It is rather because the North Korean regime—for the past half century—has locked up its people in isolation and has instilled in their minds that Kim Il Sung and Kim Jong Il are the supreme leaders of the world. Most North Korean defectors left their country because they couldn't stand living there any longer.

Kim Jong Il likes to boast that he has 200 or 300 people under his direct control. What is so great about that? If the North Korean society starts to become shaky, there is no way Kim Jong Il can maintain such a control. It is in such times of crisis within the North Korean society that U.S. and South Korean forces should enter into the North. All our forces have to do there is to maintain public order. I think it is quite ridiculous that the Japanese are concerned about a huge influx of North Korean refugees into its country. I mean, things won't go that far.

All South Korea has to do is provide some 2 million tons of rice each year to the North for a couple of years. When funds and technology start flowing into North Korea, it will achieve a high level of development in 10 years or so. Just make sure that North Koreans don't cross the border to the South for the time being. In a way, it is South Korea's responsibility to help out the North. If this happens, there is no reason why the Kim Jong Il regime cannot be overthrown. Of course, this is the responsibility of myself and North Koreans, not just of South Korea.

If North Korea walks the path of reform and liberalization (perhaps by following the Chinese model), we can proclaim an end to the Cold War era on the Korean Peninsula. Then, the two Koreas would be able to cooperate in earnest under the principle of reconciliation. In this case, adopting a federation is all right.

If this happens, it would be just like having achieved unification of the two Koreas. You see, unification does not always have to be about establishing a unified central government. Look at how the ruling and opposition parties have a falling-out with each other whenever a new government is inaugurated. This is why a central government is not always desirable or absolutely necessary in the Korean Peninsula context.

Then where should be the stronghold for advocating promotion of democracy in North Korea? The answer is South Korea. In this regard, all of you here today are not only warriors fighting for North Korea's democracy but also the vanguards of democratizing Korea as a whole.

There are many fake advocates of democracy in our society. We must fight against them. If we take the lead and initiative in strengthening the foundations of a true democracy, we will surely claim victory. This already is where history is headed for.

9

Only Regime Change Will Stop Nuclear Proliferation in North Korea

Henry S. Rowen

Henry S. Rowen is a senior fellow at the Hoover Institution and a member of Stanford University's Asia-Pacific Research Center. He is the author of Behind East Asian Growth: The Political and Social Foundations of Prosperity.

The goal of North Korea's leader Kim Jong Il is to gain enough economic resources to stay in power. As a result, North Korea has developed nuclear weapons primarily as a threat—to gain the power to extort these economic resources from other countries. North Korea began its nuclear weapons program in the late 1970s but agreed to freeze it in 1994 as part of a negotiation with the United States. However, North Korea violated its agreement and later in the 1990s started work on a new enriched uranium–based weapons program. Today, many urge the United States to make another diplomatic agreement with North Korea. However, such a solution will not work because it would depend on stringent inspection requirements that North Korea would never agree to. Instead, the United States must focus on ending the despotic regime of Kim Jong Il and on ultimately helping to create a unified, democratic Korean Peninsula.

Henry S. Rowen, "Kim Jong Il Must Go," *Policy Review*, October/November 2003.

North Korea's nuclear-weapons programs confront us with hard choices. They create a sense of urgency to make another deal with the North, but experience tells us that any new agreement will not halt the flow of crises. However we handle the immediate crisis, we will do better if we do so while having in mind an end position—something we have not done since the end of the Korean War 50 years ago. The argument here is that there should be different leadership in Pyongyang as a step towards the political unification of the peninsula.

Short of that goal, the main possibility for getting rid of the North's weapons is an agreed strategy between China and the United States. Unfortunately, there is no good evidence that this will happen.

The North's weapons pose three immediate challenges. Combined with its long-range missiles, North Korea's nuclear weapons could inflict devastation at long distances, including the United States. The threat to Japan is already rousing Tokyo to rearm. Worse still, the regime threatens to sell bombs to all comers, including terrorist organizations.

North Korea's nuclear goals

This crisis was set off by the North admitting that it had a secret nuclear-weapons program in violation of the 1994 Agreed Framework. Negotiated by the Clinton administration, the framework promised economic benefits in return for North Korea's "freezing" its nuclear program. Since breaking the agreement, the Kim Jong Il regime has loudly proclaimed that the U.S. is planning to attack and has demanded a guarantee of security from us. Perhaps seeing our campaign against Iraq has persuaded Kim that he's next. But it seems more likely that he has a different and overriding perspective.

It is to gain enough resources to stay in power. The system his father, Kim Il Sung, perfected combines extreme nationalism, severe internal repression, and a Stalinist economy. The economy's dysfunctions have led to the deaths of upwards of a million people in the past decade. Kim Jong Il's margin of survival comes from extortion. At its core are nuclear weapons—along with an implicit threat of collapse and resulting social chaos that would be costly to North Korea's neighbors.

The weapons program apparently started in the late 1970s and has continued despite several international commitments to stop it, each violated. An obvious reason for starting the program was to change the military balance on the peninsula. Although the North's conventional forces were then relatively stronger than they are now, the U.S. had both troops and nuclear weapons in the South. In 1992 we removed our weapons as part of a denuclearization agreement between North and South—one of several agreements violated by the North. The U.S. estimated that the North could soon make enough plutonium for some nuclear weapons—and might have done so already. The resulting confrontation led to the Agreed Framework in 1994, in which the North agreed to shut down its reactor and store the spent fuel (containing plutonium) under international inspection. We and others agreed to provide food and fuel, to normalize relations, and to build two large nuclear electric power reactors. (The American negotiators seemed to have assumed, not unreasonably in 1994, that the North's regime would be gone by the time the reactors were finished.)

If nuclear weapons were so important in the North's strategy, why did it agree to this freeze? Its principal source of aid, the Soviet Union, had disappeared in 1991. This, plus endemic mismanagement, threw the economy into a slump. Apparently the urgent need for food and fuel, the U.S. threat to attack North Korea's nuclear plants, and perhaps arm-twisting from China did it. (The Chinese did not sweeten the deal with food; they cut their supply in 1994–95.) The North also presumably knew something we have come to believe only since: that it had enough plutonium for a few weapons. And we now know that at some point in the 1990s it started work on a separate, enriched uranium-based weapons program, evidently with Pakistani help.

> *The weapons program apparently started in the late 1970s and has continued despite several international commitments to stop it, each violated.*

North Korea claims that we reneged on our commitments under the Agreed Framework, while the Clinton administration complained about the North's behavior. In early 2001 President Bush suspended the dialogue underway at the end of the Clinton administration, but later that year he signaled a willingness to resume talks. We were still supplying food and fuel and participating in the nuclear reactor construction program when the North revealed its second nuclear program in October 2002. In case we (and the South Koreans and Japanese) hadn't gotten the message, in April of this year [2003] the North's representative told ours that North Korea had nuclear weapons and might demonstrate (i.e., test) or sell them. In July [2003] the North announced that it had completed separating plutonium from its stored fuel rods by June 30 and that weapons production had begun. In short, North Korea is a nuclear power; on its present trajectory it will become a greater one.

> *In short, North Korea is a nuclear power; on its present trajectory it will become a greater one.*

Kim must have been severely disappointed that the hopes engendered by Clinton's diplomacy were interrupted by the harder line taken by Bush. His government says it wants a guarantee of security from us. Paranoia can't be ruled out in that nearly hermetically sealed society, in which ignorance of the West is profound. Perhaps the implications of being called a member of the "axis of evil" rattled him—although anyone other than a paranoid would see the implausibility of the U.S. attacking without South Korean agreement, which is most unlikely to be given. As for the North starting a war, there is no good reason to regard Kim as suicidal.

The Pyongyang regime has long had an ambitious goal. Fanciful as it might seem to outsiders, it is to unify the peninsula under its control; this is the purpose that justifies the regime's rigors. The U.S. is seen as the main obstacle, and no doubt Kim and company contemplate the political gap that has opened between the United States and South Korea with satisfaction.

But today Kim Jong Il is balancing fears—perhaps of a U.S. attack but surely for his fate from continued and perhaps worsening poverty. That fear is balanced against the perceived danger of opening the economy—with the latter one dominating. Since his economy can't produce many exports and with serious economic liberalization seen as too dangerous, what's left is outside help induced by threats. Although it has left the country desperately poor, the routine has worked.

Kim is often portrayed in the West as a skillful player of a weak hand. Lately, however, his play looks erratic, as [analyst] Nicholas Eberstadt has noted. He botched the creation of a special economic zone (in Sinuiju) with the Chinese and blew the opportunity to get several billion dollars soon in reparation payments from Japan by his handling of the kidnappings of Japanese citizens, and his trumpeting about nuclear weapons is helping to unify his opponents. These actions have led to cuts in the flow of fuel and food and to reports that once again the population is on the brink of famine.

He may not understand the fire with which he is playing. Building nuclear weapons puts other nations in danger, and if his having these weapons isn't enough to provoke the U.S. and perhaps the Chinese to end his rule, the prospect of North Korean fissionable material coming into the hands of terrorists should do it.

North Korea's poverty

This is a strikingly poor country for one populated by disciplined and well-educated Koreans. The ending of Russian aid and a cut in Chinese subsidies after 1990 contributed to economic output and foreign trade declining by about one-third and to a food supply deficit of over one million tons a year. Food conditions became disastrous in 1994 and 1995. The authorities diverted food to the army, party cadres, and workers in key industries, leaving the rest to fend for themselves. Probably upwards of a million people (around 4 percent of the population) died.

Agriculture is still collectivized 25 years after the Chinese started to abandon this mode of production. A measure of its condition was that family garden plots (limited to 120 square yards per family) yielded one-third of all agricultural output in 1997. More important in that highly industrialized economy is the sorry state of industry. Goods are shoddy and scarce. Many factories lie idle and productivity is low. Poverty is overwhelming. Per capita GDP [gross domestic product] seems to be about $700, for a national total of around $13 billion to $15 billion. The regime's core supporters get a large share of the country's meager supply of goods (partly through access to hard currency), a supply that might now be on the verge of inadequacy even for the elite. The military has long absorbed about one-fourth of the total, an extraordinary share for an impoverished country. Allowing for the sustenance of other parts of the core, perhaps $7 billion to $9 billion is left for the remaining 21 million people, around $300–$400 per year per person, an amount available for such little investment as occurs as well as personal consumption. The World Food Program estimates that 57 percent of the population is malnourished, including 45 percent of children under the age of five. No wonder people try to flee.

Cash from exports and goods in kind from outside provide the crucial margin for the regime's survival. Until recently, these probably ran about $2 billion per year. They have come from six main sources: exports of raw materials, the export of weapons and drugs, gifts from Koreans in Japan, fuel oil supplied under the 1994 Agreed Framework, other support from China and South Korea (for example, via the Mount Kumgang project for South Korean tourists), and gifts of food from many countries. There have also been secret payments from the South. According to the public prosecutor, South Korean President Kim Dae Jung paid Kim Jong Il $100 million as the ticket price for the June 2000 summit meeting in Pyongyang. The Hyundai Corporation paid an additional $350 million, supposedly for business purposes. Today, most if not all of these sources are diminished, leaving the regime in even more difficulty than usual.

Kim Dae Jung may have seen his Sunshine Policy of payments to the North as encouraging economic reform, but they had the opposite effect: Money supplied without conditions weakens the incentive to change. Such gifts don't solve economic problems; they only leave the country in a precarious state that causes it repeatedly to go to the brink.

> **Some market-oriented reforms notwithstanding, there is little evidence of a willingness to undertake basic ones.**

The economy would benefit greatly if the million-man army were to be scaled way back. The recent statement by Pyongyang that its nuclear weapons enable it to shrink its huge army has a logic. But this is North Korea, where the army is at the core of the regime, and its ability to threaten Seoul is one of its two main assets, the other being nuclear weapons. It is hard to imagine unilateral cutbacks if there is an opportunity to get paid for cutting back. Even then, one doubts that any such agreement would long be honored.

Steps toward liberalization

The survival of this island of poverty and obscurantism in one of the world's most prosperous and dynamic regions is a tribute to the sturdiness of the Korean people, to the power of juche (its ideology of self-reliant ultranationalism), and to totalitarian controls. Collapse of Soviet rule and the fate of the Ceaucescus[1] in Romania supply nightmares to the North's rulers. More ambiguous is the model of China. The Chinese Communist Party's great economic success must have appeal, but after Kim returned from China in 2000, where the splendid results of its liberalization were on display, North Korean television described China's "opening" as a "Trojan horse tasked with destabilizing socialism." As [analyst] Marcus Noland has noted, Kim does not want to risk being "destabilized."

Nonetheless, some liberalizing steps have been taken, including creating free trade zones (Rajin-Sonbong and Sinuiju—both bungled) and allowing farmers' markets. Potentially important is a recent large increase in the official price of goods (40,000–60,000 percent for grains). Given that wages are being changed differently for various groups in the society, there will be significant winners and losers from this "reform."

Some market-oriented reforms notwithstanding, there is little evidence of a willingness to undertake basic ones. Juche is one explanation for this reluctance to liberalize, but there are others. Kim and his core supporters must perceive their tenure as being more fragile than have the Chinese leaders; hence a stronger insistence on keeping control. And their initiatives have been extraordinarily inept. Outsiders often comment on the ignorance of Northern officials about the world economy and how markets work.

Widespread expectations through the mid-1990s of an early collapse, especially after Kim Il Sung's death in 1994, have been succeeded by the belief that Kim Jong Il's rule will be lim-

---

1. Nicolae Ceausescu was the president of Romania until 1989, when an anti-Communist rebellion ended his regime. He and his wife were condemned to death by a military court and executed.

ited only by his longevity—and that one of his sons might succeed him. This view arguably weighs too little the effects of life at the margin of starvation for many people, meager resources for many core supporters, and increasing knowledge of the people about the outside world. An appropriate image is that of a gambler who every year faces a significant, perhaps now increasing, chance of ruin.

Alternatives to Kim's rule

The unlikelihood that Kim Jong Il will preside over a basic economic transformation, together with his nuclear brinkmanship, leads to the question of an alternative to Kim dynasty rule. Internal political relations there are obscure. Because years passed before Kim Jong Il assumed some of the trappings of power, some outsiders assumed that he was not firmly in charge. That view seems wrong. Evidently he was powerful in the last decade of his father's life, and his rule seems to have been unchallenged since then.

The two most salient institutions are the Korean Workers Party and the army. As far as one can tell (which is not very far), Kim is firmly in charge of both. The Workers Party has its functions in the spheres of ideology and population control, but it doesn't seem able to act independently. In contrast, the army does have power. It has the guns. No doubt Kim has taken pains to keep this power from being concentrated in the persons of a few generals. Nonetheless, if conditions get bad enough, members of these elites might act against Kim.

> *South Koreans have long worried about a collapse of the North's government.*

Worries often expressed about regime "collapse" assume that no political alternative to the Kim dynasty could succeed without political chaos—this in a country with nuclear weapons. That might be so but shouldn't simply be assumed. If conditions get bad enough, might someone who understands the need for basic economic change seize power in a way analogous to Park Chung Hee's takeover in South Korea or Deng Xiaoping's succession to the Gang of Four in China? Both were dictators who, by opening their countries, produced rapid growth and, as a consequence, increased personal freedoms for their peoples—and for South Korea, democracy. As Deng told [former U.S. secretary of state] George Shultz in July 1988 when asked his opinion of [President Mikhail] Gorbachev's reforms in the Soviet Union, "He's got it backwards. He opened up the political system without a clue about the economy. The result is chaos. I did it the other way around, starting in agriculture and small businesses, where opening up worked, so now I have a demand for more of what succeeds." What about political opening? "That will come later and will start small, just as in the economy. You have to be patient but you have to get the sequence right.". . .

The interests of South Korea

Until circa 1990, one could fairly say that American and South Korean interests were congruent: Both were about the security of the South and its consolidation of democracy. The robustness of Korean democracy is no longer in doubt. The problem is security. Of course both want to avert war, but Americans (and Japanese and apparently Chinese) perceive greater dangers from the North's missile and nuclear weapons than do South Koreans. Southerners (rightly or wrongly) do not expect the North's missiles or nuclear weapons to land on them, nor do they see themselves as the target of nuclear-armed terrorists. Americans see themselves as threatened both ways.

South Koreans have long worried about a collapse of the North's government. They fear millions of people coming south and the burden of financing construction of the North's economy. Many use the costly unification of Germany as a reason (or perhaps rationalization) for keeping the status quo. In any case, a large amount of outside capital would be needed (large relative to the South's economy but not in relation to world capital flows). As Marcus Noland notes in *Avoiding the Apocalypse* a capital transfer of $300 billion to $500 billion could bring per capita incomes in the North to 60 percent of the South's level within 10 years. Although the long-run payoff to the people in the southern part of a unified Korea from a prosperous North would be high both economically and politically, there would be costs in between. Assuming that most of this capital would come from the South, growth there would be depressed during that decade by perhaps 1 percent a year.

Here the U.S. has been neglectful. It is in our interest to commit now to helping the South with this financial burden if the North's regime collapses.

The Roh Moo-Hyun government [of South Korea] needs to decide on its goals. It cannot act as a middleman between the U.S and the North. It needs to choose how much it values the American alliance versus helping to sustain a regime that threatens Seoul with destruction, whose military programs are rousing the Japanese to rearm, that sells missiles to all comers, and that might sell nuclear weapons.

The interests of China, Japan, and Russia

China's position is likely to be pivotal. Its leaders don't want to see a communist regime collapse; they don't want a flood of refugees coming to China; they don't want a war that would bring down the regime and might bring American forces to the Yalu; they don't want to see a rearmed Japan, especially a nuclear-armed one; and they want good relations with the United States. Nonetheless, they seem to be leaving the job of stopping it largely to us.

China's apparent lack of vigor might simply reflect a reluctance to tackle forcefully a fellow communist-ruled state many of whose senior officials are old comrades. Or might it be based on the view that the Americans and others will pay to solve it? Or, more ominously, might China judge that U.S.-South Korean differences will preclude war, that they will speed the departure of American forces from the mainland of Asia, and that Japan is no longer a major force? Whatever the combination of views in Beijing, a failure to act decisively could leave China with three more nuclear-armed neighbors—two in Korea plus Japan—along with other troubles.

The mirror image of the putative Chinese view—"Let the Americans solve it"—is an American one: "Let the Chinese solve it." Why is this not mainly a Chinese problem, on the view that they have more to lose than anyone else from a nuclear-armed Northeast Asia? That might be so if it were not for the North's possible sale of bomb materials. A more considered view is that we have enough shared interests with the Chinese to try jointly to solve the problem of the North.

The Chinese long claimed that they had little influence in Pyongyang. Relations between their leaders have been cool to frigid, but with China its principal supplier of food and fuel as well as the main obstacle to the flight of refugees, that position lacked credibility. Its supplies now are even more crucial to the regime's survival than in the past. And if China agreed not to return refugees but rather to send them on, and if South Korea (and the U.S.) agreed to take more of them, there would likely be a rush for the exit. One refugee has said that the cities would empty in six months. For a horde of Koreans to arrive and stay in China is a nightmare for Beijing, but a position well short of threatening to empty the North of people—with refugees passing through to elsewhere—would put great pressure on Pyongyang.

The Chinese are edging towards doing more. Recently they let it be known that they cut off the North's fuel supply for 72 hours. They might come to see what is happening as sufficiently hazardous to warrant strong action. For instance, how do they regard the possibility of the North selling readily fissionable materials or fabricated bombs to anyone who pays enough? Is it beyond the bounds of possibility that such things could come into the hands of Uigher terrorists?

The Chinese have, to little avail, been telling Kim Jong Il to adopt the kinds of reforms that are transforming their economy. Perhaps they say (only to each other?) that what North Korea needs is a leader of the "Deng Xiaoping" sort. Worries are expressed in both South Korea and China about a Romanian-type regime collapse in the North, but too little attention has been given to a change in rulers within the same political structure. If they are sufficiently motivated, the Chinese are best positioned to bring it off.

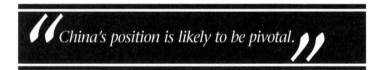

China's position is likely to be pivotal.

Notwithstanding the speculations above on why China might not act decisively against the North, there is arguably a large overlapping interest with the United States. China's comparative advantage is in squeezing the North while that of the U.S. is in rounding up support from others and, if necessary, offering some kind of non-attack commitment.

If the Chinese decide to move against Kim, might they try for a larger goal: to try to engineer a peaceful unification of a non-nuclear, democratic Korea on condition that the Americans leave? Considering how we got there in the first place (to defend against an attack by a communist North backed by Soviet and Chinese power), that could look like not a bad outcome. . . .

As for Japan, the firing of a North Korean missile over that country in 1998 was a deeply disturbing event, to which is now added its nuclear weapons. There is also popular outrage at the North's kidnapping of Japanese citizens. These events are having consequences. The Japanese are doing R&D [research and development] on ballistic missile defenses and are considering building them. There are reports about Japanese air and naval forces being given offensive weapons. Japan would probably participate in a multilateral maritime weapons interdiction effort against the North, especially if approved by the United Nations. Talk about Japan getting nuclear weapons is still confined to the political fringe, but that could change if North Korea continues with its programs.

This crisis brings to the fore our role in the defense of Japan. So far we have been unable to assure the safety of Japan against North Korean threats; hence the growth in the attitude that Japan has to do more for itself. A big cut in our forces in Korea would have repercussions in Japan, and their total withdrawal even more so. Much would depend on the context. Our leaving in anything like the present situation would create alarm. On the other hand, a reduction or even withdrawal associated with the creation of a unified, democratic, non-nuclear Korea would be much less alarming. But even in so favorable a case, a new U.S.-Japan security formula would be needed. For now, the Japanese still hope the U.S. will solve this problem, and they are willing to help.

Russia is likely to remain a marginal player. It has as normal diplomatic relations as any country has with the North. Their trade is small. However, trade between a unified, capitalist Korea and the Russian Far East could become large and of great mutual benefit.

The dangers of negotiating with North Korea

Today, there are many advocates of a deal that can be labeled Agreed Framework Mark II. One can guess at its contents. It would, again, entail promises by the North to forgo nuclear programs in exchange for benefits. These would include food and fuel—but surely not completing the two nuclear reactors under construction as part of the 1994 Agreed Framework. It might also include cuts in conventional forces. (Having the North's army merely move back from the DMZ [the demilitarized zone between North and South Korea] wouldn't accomplish much because it could quickly be returned.) The North is pressing for a commitment by the United States not to attack. This is less innocuous than it might seem. The threat here is a point of leverage in what is likely to be an ongoing series of confrontations, and given the North's record, we could find ourselves having to attack in self-defense. Suppose the North is found to be supplying nuclear weapons to [terrorist group] al Qaeda?

> *That anything like the Kim dynasty is doomed should not be in doubt.*

The North's obligations would entail much more pervasive inspection and the removal of readily fissile materials (those which are found, that is) from the country. If this course is pursued, it would likely also include specific and closely monitored economic opening actions that would bring in outsiders—presumably South Koreans—widely throughout the country as well as specific actions on human rights.

To those who will inevitably argue that such demands would be rejected by the North and, anyway, the main aim is to stop the weapons programs, the response is: You have a good chance of not stopping the weapons; there will be other crises; we need a basic change in the North; and we can offer the North more benefits (i.e., money) to go with these demands.

The nuclear inspection task would be formidable, especially for fabricated weapons. The only way to have confidence that they are not present in a country known to have had them (e.g., South Africa) is for the country to be sufficiently open that insiders with knowledge can safely reveal cheating. That condition will not exist in Kim Jong Il's North Korea. The American effort to round up international support for inspecting and seizing exports of missiles and drugs at least puts pressure on the North in the maneuvering for an agreement. An economic blockade (excepting perhaps some food) might bring Kim down, and might be supported in the Security Council if proposed by the U.S. and China, but that brings us back to how far China is willing to go.

If something like an Agreed Framework Mark II is reached, there will be celebrations over having averted a great danger. One should not be too ready to carp at whatever emerges; this is a problem from hell. But elation would be premature. The inspection requirements for confidence that the fissile material production programs—and any fabricated bombs—are gone are so stringent as to be unlikely to be met, and as Pyongyang demonstrated recently, the inspectors could be thrown out at any time. It is axiomatic that any government headed by Kim Jong Il will have nuclear weapons, despite any agreement signed by his government (unless the Chinese take decisive action).

Therefore, we should aim to have a leadership in Pyongyang committed to developing the country, rather than surviving on nuclear extortion, as a step towards the political unification of the peninsula. This implies the end of the Kim dynasty. Since the end of the Korean War we have accepted the division and constant tensions, interspersed with crises, as inevitable. We have reacted to events instead of creating them. It is too dangerous to keep doing this.

Some suggested initiatives

We should undertake several initiatives as a part of or—to the extent we have not tied our hands in a negotiation—independently of any agreement.

Try to reach agreement with China on a strategy for eliminating the North's weapons. The Bush administration would have to trust China to deliver on a promise to rid the North of weapons and China would have to trust that the U.S. would deliver a (rather unpalatable, from the American perspective) package of concessions. But, to repeat, there are no good options.

Undertake a serious human rights campaign. Make human rights a major topic with the North—and in public. Focusing only on nuclear weapons enables Kim to beat the drum of nationalism and to avoid addressing his manifest domestic failings.

This effort should include the free exchange of people, religious liberty, open borders, and family reunification, as the recent joint "Statement of Principles for U.S.–North Korean Relations" urged (*Wall Street Journal*, January 18, 2003). Having recently expanded Korean-language broadcasting, we should do more to distribute information on human rights abuses and to investigate religious persecution. On refugees, we should press Russia and especially China to process refugee claims, press the UNCHR to invoke its treaty with China on access to refugees, and pass the bill in Congress granting North Korean refugees the same rights as Cubans.

Promote specific economic reforms. If we (meaning the coalition we are trying to form) end up supplying economic aid, some of it should be conditioned on specific liberalizing action in certain sectors, as Adam Garfinkle has argued in the *New Republic* (November 4, 2002). The principle should be "pay for performance." We should also be willing to help in educating North Koreans on markets and rule-of-law reforms. Given the minuscule size of the North's economy, the cost of the aid should not be much of an issue; the question is what we get for the money.

Work to find a successor to Kim. Several of the items discussed above would advance this aim. In addition, we should try to identify a potential North Korean "Deng Xiaoping" or a "Park Chung Hee." How this might be done is, of course, a large question, but one begins by identifying the need. Probably only China could engineer this—if anyone can.

At the end of a transition (which might be short), the aim is to have a peacefully united and democratic Korea without nuclear weapons, the North's top leaders retired, a rapidly developing North supported by outside investment, and perhaps a U.S. security linkage. That last decision should depend not only on Korean preferences, but also on how we then assess our role in Northeast Asian security.

That anything like the Kim dynasty is doomed should not be in doubt. The forces of economic and political liberalism are too powerful. The question is when and how it goes and what disasters occur before then. The time is late for us to be thinking about how to make it go away peacefully.

10

Regime Change Will Not Stop Nuclear Proliferation in North Korea

Friends Committee on National Legislation

The Friends Committee on National Legislation is a public interest lobby founded in 1943 by members of the Religious Society of Friends (also called Quakers).

Some Bush administration officials believe that North Korea's leader Kim Jong Il is not a trustworthy negotiating partner and are convinced that military action or regime change will be necessary to stop nuclear proliferation by the country. Regime change could be accomplished by imposing economic sanctions or by encouraging the flow of North Korean refugees. However, regime change without international approval violates international law and would only result in increased instability. The collapse of North Korea's government would cause devastating consequences, including tens of thousands of deaths. It also could result in North Korea selling its stockpiles of nuclear weapons to the highest bidders, including terrorist organizations. North Korea's collapse would therefore decrease U.S. security, not increase it.

Some Bush Administration officials say that North Korea's leader, Kim Jong Il is not a trustworthy negotiating partner. They conclude that the U.S. will not be safe from North Korea

Friends Committee on National Legislation, "Why Regime Change Is Not the Answer: Talking Points on North Korea," www.fcnl.org, September 10, 2003. Copyright © 2003 by Friends Committee on National Legislation. Reproduced by permission.

as long as Kim Jong Il remains in power. For those officials, negotiations are no more than milestones to pass while traveling on the road to greater confrontation. After the Six-Party talks[1] in August 2003, the *Wall Street Journal* quoted a U.S. official: "We're letting them dig their own grave." The "other measures" frequently alluded to by the U.S. Administration could mean a U.S. military attack on North Korea, including a nuclear attack. Or "other measures" could mean attempting to force North Korea's collapse through squeezing it economically. Yet war with North Korea or forced regime change would decrease U.S. security. Negotiations are the best way to address the most urgent potential threat posed by North Korea, as well as the best way to promote long-term change.

War with North Korea would not make the United States safer

North Korea may already possess nuclear weapons, or may be in the process of developing them. Is war the best way to protect the U.S. from this potential threat? A military strike of North Korea's nuclear power plant could not be made without releasing clouds of radiation over South Korea and Japan, as well as provoking a military response from North Korea that could leave tens of thousands of people dead in a matter of weeks. A prolonged war on the Korean peninsula would be costly, and result in hundreds of thousands of deaths, including the deaths of some of the 100,000 U.S. troops based in Asia and the tens of thousands of U.S. citizens living in Seoul. War with North Korea could well move beyond the Korean peninsula, involving China and Japan as well. Economic consequences could be ruinous for U.S. businesses. Preventing war with North Korea is essential, and is well within the power of the United States. North Korea has repeatedly asked for a nonaggression agreement from the U.S. A non-aggression agreement between North Korea and the U.S., and including South Korea, China, Japan and Russia was discussed at the August 2003 Six-Party talks.

Since the risks of war with North Korea are well known, military action is rarely openly proposed. Instead, members of the Administration and Congress hint at regime change caused

---

1. The six parties who participated in the talks were North Korea, the United States, China, South Korea, Japan, and Russia.

through squeezing North Korea economically, or through encouraging the flow of North Korean refugees. For one nation to seek regime change in another nation without following an international decision-making process is a violation of international law, and for that reason alone such a tactic should not be pursued. . . .

> *Negotiations are the best way to address the most urgent potential threat posed by North Korea, as well as the best way to promote long-term change.*

As the world witnessed in Iraq, regime change does not come easily and can result in increased instability. This would be even more the case in North Korea, where people have long been prepared for an assault, and mistrust of the outside world is deep-seated. A collapse could have far-reaching humanitarian consequences far beyond either China or South Korea's ability to meet such an emergency. Tens of thousands of people could die in the aftermath. The administration has acknowledged that failed states create the conditions for producing terrorists. Furthermore, senior military officials in the United States Forces in Korea (USFK) have admitted off the record that it would take years to find and secure existing stockpiles of known chemical weapons and suspected biological weapons, let alone any nuclear material, regardless of whether North Korea collapses or is defeated in war. Such material could be sold across borders to the highest bidder, including terrorist organizations, increasing threats to the U.S. and the rest of the world. North Korea's collapse would decrease U.S. security, not increase it.

Only negotiation will work

At the end of December 2002, as North Korea's relations with the U.S. deteriorated, North Korea kicked out the International Atomic Energy Agency (IAEA) inspectors that had been overseeing the suspension of North Korea's nuclear power plant. With the inspectors gone, North Korea is free to pursue reprocessing the spent fuel to produce nuclear weapons material. North Korea has announced that the reprocessing has already taken place; U.S. intelligence has not been able to unambiguously confirm or disprove their claim. As already stated, a military strike cannot safely bomb nuclear material out of existence. Instead, North Korea must agree to give up their program, and inspectors must be allowed to verify that the program has been dismantled and that nuclear material, including plutonium separated in 2003, is safely stored and ultimately removed from the country. Negotiations can result in an agreement that would verifiably refreeze North Korea's plutonium program. Negotiations have the potential to achieve this far more quickly than war or regime change. North Korea has indicated its willingness to give up its nuclear weapons program if the U.S. changes its "hostile policy" and does not impede economic dealings with South Korea and Japan.

> *North Korea's collapse would decrease U.S. security, not increase it.*

The most challenging aspect of North Korea's nuclear weapons program is the heavily enriched uranium (HEU) program. There is evidence that in the late 1990s, North Korea was exploring such a program. Although there is great ambiguity about the extent of North Korea's HEU program, the program is thought to be years away from producing weapons. However, HEU processing is much easier to conceal than a plutonium program. An inspection process capable of verifying the extent of North Korea's HEU program and its dismantlement will be difficult to negotiate. In addition, negotiators must agree on an adequate program for inspecting pre-1994 plutonium production. As with suspected stores of chemical weapons, there is little knowledge about where all aspects of an HEU program might be hidden in North Korea. The program could be continued covertly in the chaos of a post-war or post-collapse environment.

North Koreans must be given many more opportunities to interact and learn from the rest of the world so that individuals can develop their own perspectives. Within its own borders, North Korea is responsible for violations of human rights, including re-education camps where many die for political crimes. Change in North Korea must come from within. Yet North Koreans know very little of the outside world and are unable to compare North Korea with other countries. They are very suspicious of outside intervention, particularly from the U.S. Despite the recent nuclear crisis, the North Korean government continues to send officials and academics to other countries for training in a range of topics, including agriculture, medicine, market economies and information technology. Even top leaders in North Korea are eager to learn more about the outside world; recently appointed North Korean Minister Pak Nam Gil said on a recent trip to South Korea, "It's a pity I have only two eyes so I can't see more in such a short time." Measures taken to force North Korea's collapse would result in North Korea closing its doors.

11

A U.S. Attack Will Not Destroy North Korea's Nuclear Capabilities

Michael Levi

Michael Levi is a fellow in foreign policy studies at the Brookings Institution, a nonprofit public policy research institution. He previously served as the director of the Federation of American Scientists' Strategic Security Project.

A U.S. strike on North Korean nuclear targets will not eliminate North Korea's nuclear production capacity. Precision bombing could hit Yongbyon, North Korea, the location of one of the country's nuclear reactors as well as a plutonium reprocessing facility without causing much radioactive fallout. However, the United States does not know the site of North Korea's clandestine uranium-enrichment program. Furthermore, it is possible that North Korea has built other undetected plutonium reprocessing facilities beyond Yongbyon. It is therefore impossible for the U.S. military to denuclearize North Korea without occupying the country.

President Bush caused barely a ripple on March 3 [2003] when he apparently shifted America's North Korea policy, remarking to reporters that if America's efforts "don't work diplomatically, they'll have to work militarily." And Bush's words may signify a broader shift. As the Korean crisis has escalated, more and more analysts—including some in the Bush administration—have begun arguing that a U.S. strike on North Korean nuclear targets may be worth the risk.

Many of these analysts believe the United States can strike without prompting a broader war, and they predict that the risks of lethal nuclear fallout from such a precision attack on North Korea's known nuclear sites may be minimal. But they are ignoring one critical problem: In 1994, when North Korea's program was restricted to three nuclear reactors plus the reprocessing of plutonium at Yongbyon, we might have been able to effectively eliminate it through precision strikes. By contrast, the current crisis stems from last October's [2002] revelation of North Korea's clandestine uranium-enrichment program, the location of which is unknown. Thus, eliminating Pyongyang's nuclear production capacity through precision bombing is now virtually impossible.

Fallout could be contained

Target number one in a precision strike would be North Korea's reprocessing facility at Yongbyon, where plutonium is extracted from spent nuclear fuel for use in nuclear weapons. The only technological hurdle would be preventing the spread of radioactive fallout. And the good news for any such plan is that massive radioactive fallout is unlikely: A U.S. strike would almost certainly avoid dispersing more than a small fraction of North Korea's radioactive materials, and even this fallout would be largely contained within Yongbyon.

> *The larger problem is not that Yongbyon can't be bombed for safety reasons; it's that North Korea contains other nuclear sites that the United States can't bomb because we don't know where they are.*

Why would fallout be contained? Inspectors saw the facility when it was roughly half finished in 1992, and American intelligence is thus able to infer what the completed plant looks like. Using this information, a careful strike that minimizes fallout should be possible. As a senior Clinton administration scientist told *The New Republic*, "There are likely to be ways to destroy the reprocessing plant without causing major fires and using the collapse of the heavy concrete walls to trap most of the radioactive material in the rubble, thus avoiding serious fallout at distances much beyond the Yongbyon site itself." Another knowledgeable source confirms this, adding that the radioactive mess localized to Yongbyon could be a bonus, making it difficult for the North Koreans to return and salvage valuable materials, including spent fuel rods.

> **Complete denuclearization of North Korea . . . is impossible militarily short of occupying the North.**

The other priority target would be North Korea's nuclear reactor, also at Yongbyon, which, remembering Chernobyl, people tend to assume could not be hit without a major radiological catastrophe. Careful analysis, however, shows the reactor could be struck with little risk of major fallout. North Korea's reactor is fueled with natural uranium, a toxic but barely radioactive material. As the reactor operates, nuclear fission converts the uranium to more radioactive substances; thus, the longer the reactor has been operating, the greater the danger of radiological dispersal. Since North Korea refueled its reactor with natural uranium before restarting it barely a month ago, the risk is greatly reduced. According to the Clinton administration scientist, "A direct attack on the reactor now, before it has operated for very long with its fresh fuel load, might not spread very much high-level radioactive material." According to another knowledgeable source, detailed calculations have shown that even in a worst-case scenario—high winds, a hot graphite fire that would loft radioactive materials high in the air so they might be carried far, and a reactor that had been operating for a long time—there would be no danger beyond North Korea's borders and no immediate radiation sicknesses or fatalities beyond Yongbyon.

The locations of North Korea's nuclear facilities are unknown

It's true, of course, that no attack would be risk-free, even discounting the potential for North Korean retaliation. Small amounts of fallout would be detectable in South Korea, where the p.r. [public relations] crisis could be far worse for the United States than the public health one. But the larger problem is not that Yongbyon can't be bombed for safety reasons; it's that North Korea contains other nuclear sites that the United States can't bomb because we don't know where they are. Since the United States last considered air strikes, in 1994, our knowledge of North Korea's nuclear landscape has greatly deteriorated. Indeed, the current crisis started in October 2002, when the administration disclosed for the first time its knowledge of North Korea's clandestine uranium-enrichment program. Though it might be more than a year before this program yields enough material for a bomb, our knowledge of the program is so uncertain that we cannot discount the possibility that it will be successful sooner. And, unlike the reprocessing at Yongbyon, the location of the uranium program is entirely unknown. Our evidence of North Korea's enrichment program is its purchasing of centrifuge equipment and associated materials, not satellite imagery of an enrichment plant. The problem is much like in Iraq, where the world can rightly insist that [dictator Saddam Hussein] has chemical weapons without being able to point inspectors to their locations. And, since, like a chemical plant, a centrifuge program consumes little electricity and can be physically small, American intelligence is unlikely to locate it. It is thus almost certain that any precision strike on North Korea's nuclear facilities will leave some of its uranium-enrichment program intact.

And hidden enrichment activity is not our only blind spot. In *Disarming Strangers*, Leon V. Sigal recounts that the possible presence of undetected plutonium-reprocessing facilities beyond Yongbyon was a crucial point of debate among American military planners in 1994. Today, North Korea is even more likely than in 1994 to have covert reprocessing facilities, potentially making a strike on Yongbyon even less comprehensive and, thus, less useful. Like enrichment plants, reprocessing facilities require little physical space or electricity to operate and are therefore very hard to detect. We have minimal ability to monitor their construction above ground, and the North Koreans, master tunnelers, may well have built underground, making detection all but impossible. In theory, plutonium reprocessing can be detected by mechanically sniffing for krypton-85, a gas produced by reprocessing. But emissions from Japan's and China's legitimate reprocessing facilities could drown out those from a covert North Korean program. During the 1994 crisis, some within the Clinton administration tried to rectify this by pushing for the emplacement of at least a dozen krypton-85 detectors inside North Korea. But such intrusive verification was deemed by American negotiators to be too offensive to the North Koreans, and the detector idea was scrapped, meaning that today the same uncertainty over covert facilities persists.

It would be nice if President Bush's view of the military option—if America's efforts "don't work diplomatically, they'll have to work militarily"—were accurate. But no amount of wishing will change the facts on the ground, and those facts dictate that what might be possible diplomatically—complete denuclearization of North Korea—is impossible militarily short of occupying the North. In 1994, military action, though unpalatable, was a genuine alternative for achieving the same objective sought by diplomacy. Unfortunately, it no longer is.

12

Multilateral Negotiations Are Needed to Stop North Korea's Nuclear Program

James T. Laney and Jason T. Shaplen

James T. Laney served as U.S. ambassador to South Korea from 1993 to 1997. He also is president emeritus of Emory University and cochairman of an independent task force on managing change on the Korean Peninsula, sponsored by the Council on Foreign Relations. Jason T. Shaplen was policy adviser at the Korean Peninsula Energy Development Organization from 1995 to 1999 and is a member of the Council on Foreign Relations task force.

North Korea's actions in 2002 and 2003, particularly its decision to restart its frozen plutonium-based nuclear program, have created a dangerous crisis. Resolving this crisis will require multilateral efforts. The United States, China, Japan, Russia, and South Korea must agree to guarantee North Korea's security. In addition, the countries involved will need to provide North Korea with economic aid. Once North Korea has been assured the security it has supposedly been seeking, it must end its nuclear programs and allow immediate and continuous inspections by the International Atomic Energy Agency. North Korea must also end its missile program and sales, reduce its ground troops along the demilitarized zone, and implement economic reforms. Timing will be crucial to the success of this two-stage multilateral process.

James T. Laney and Jason T. Shaplen, "How to Deal with North Korea," *Foreign Affairs*, vol. 82, March/April 2003, p. 16. Copyright © 2003 by the Council on Foreign Relations, Inc. Reproduced by permission.

> If North Korea restarts its plutonium reprocessing facil-
> ity, it could produce four or five nuclear weapons
> within six months.

P rogress in reducing tensions on the Korean Peninsula, never
easy, has reached a dangerous impasse. [In 2002 and 2003
the world] witnessed an extraordinary series of events in the region that have profound implications for security and stability
throughout Northeast Asia, a region that is home to 100,000
U.S. troops and three of the world's 12 largest economies.

North Korea's actions

Perhaps the most dramatic of these events was North Korea's
December [2002] decision to restart its frozen plutonium-based
nuclear program at Yongbyon—including a reprocessing facility that separates plutonium for nuclear weapons from spent
reactor fuel. Just as disturbing was the North's stunning public
admission two months earlier that it had begun building a
new, highly-enriched-uranium (HEU) nuclear program. And
then came yet another unsettling development: a growing,
sharp division emerged between the United States and the new
South Korean government over how to respond.

But recent events have not been entirely negative. In the
two months prior to the October [2002], HEU revelation, North
Korea had, with remarkable speed, undertaken an important
series of positive initiatives that seemed the polar opposite of
its posturing on the nuclear issue. These included initiating an
unscheduled meeting between its foreign minister, Paek Nam
Sun, and Secretary of State Colin Powell in July—the highest-
level contact between the two nations since the Bush administration took office; inviting a U.S. delegation for talks in Pyongyang; proposing the highest-level talks with South Korea in a
year; agreeing to re-establish road and rail links with the South
and starting work on the project almost immediately; demi-
ning portions of the demilitarized zone (DMZ) [marking the
boundary between North and South Korea] and wide corridors
on the east and west coasts surrounding the rail links; sending
more than 600 athletes and representatives to join the Asian
Games in Pusan, South Korea (marking the North's first-ever
participation in an international sporting event in the South);
enacting a series of economic and market reforms (including
increasing wages, allowing the price of staples to float freely,

and inaugurating a special economic zone similar to those in China); restarting the highest-level talks with Japan in two years; holding a subsequent summit with Japanese Prime Minister Junichiro Koizumi, during which Pyongyang admitted abducting Japanese citizens in the 1970s and 1980s; and finally, allowing the surviving abductees to visit Japan.

Viewed individually, let alone together, North Korea's initiatives represented the most promising signs of change on the peninsula in decades. Whether by desire or by necessity, the North finally appeared to be responding to the long-standing concerns of the United States, South Korea, and Japan. Equally important, Pyongyang seemed to have abandoned its policy of playing Washington, Seoul, and Tokyo off one another by addressing the concerns of one while ignoring those of the other two. For the first time, the North was actively (even aggressively) engaging all three capitals simultaneously.

The U.S. response

Until October [2002], that is, when North Korea acknowledged the existence of its clandestine HEU program—ending the diplomatic progress instantly. Once the news broke, Pyongyang quickly offered to halt the HEU program in exchange for a nonaggression pact with the United States. But Washington, unwilling to reward bad behavior, initially refused to open a dialogue unless the North first abandoned its HEU effort. In November, the United States went a step further: saying that Pyongyang had violated the 1994 Agreed Framework and several other nuclear nonproliferation pacts, Washington engineered the suspension of deliveries of the 500,000 tons of heavy fuel oil sent to the North each year under the 1994 accord. The Agreed Framework had frozen the North's plutonium program—a program that had included a five-megawatt experimental reactor, two larger reactors under construction, and the reprocessing facility—narrowly averting a catastrophic war on the Korean Peninsula.

In the weeks following the suspension of fuel shipments, the United States hardened its stance against dialogue with the North—despite the fact that most U.S. allies were encouraging a diplomatic solution to the situation. North Korea responded by announcing plans to reopen its Yongbyon facilities. It immediately removed the seals and monitoring cameras from its frozen nuclear labs and reactors and, a few days later, began to move its dangerous spent fuel rods out of storage. Pyongyang subsequently announced its intention to reopen the critical reprocessing plant in February 2003. On December 31, it expelled the inspectors of the International Atomic Energy Agency (IAEA). And on January 9, it announced its withdrawal from the nuclear Nonproliferation Treaty.

> *Although Bush administration officials insist otherwise, it is possible, as North Korean officials have suggested, that Pyongyang decided to step up its nuclear program in response to what it perceived as Washington's increasingly hostile attitude.*

Although Washington, strongly urged by Seoul and Tokyo, ultimately agreed to talks, the situation appeared to be worsening almost daily. Depending on how it is resolved, the standoff could still prove a positive turning point in resolving one of the world's most dangerous flash points. But it could also lead to an even worse crisis than in 1994. The proper approach, therefore, is to now re-engage with North Korea without rewarding it for bad behavior. Working together, the major external interested parties (China, Japan, Russia, and the United States) should jointly and officially guarantee the security of the entire Korean Peninsula. But the outside powers should also insist that Pyongyang abandon its nuclear weapons program before offering it any enticements. Only when security has been established (and verified by intrusive, regular inspections) should a prearranged comprehensive deal be implemented—one that involves extensive reforms in the North, an increase in aid and investment, and, eventually, a Korean federation.

The history of North Korea's nuclear program

To understand how the most promising signs of progress in decades quickly deteriorated into nuclear brinkmanship, it is necessary to first understand the origins and motivation behind the North's HEU program and Pyongyang's subsequent decision to restart its plutonium program. Even before North Korea admitted that it was building a new HEU program, the United States had long suspected the country of violating its relevant international commitments. Three years ago, such concerns had led to U.S. inspections of suspicious underground facilities in Kumchang-ni. Although those inspections did not reveal any actual treaty violations—in part because Pyongyang had ample time to remove evidence before the inspectors arrived—suspicions lingered. These doubts proved justified in July 2002, when the United States conclusively confirmed the existence of the North's HEU program.

It now seems likely that Pyongyang actually started its HEU program in 1997 or 1998. Although [President] Kim Jong Il's motives for doing so will probably never be clear (his regime has a record of confounding observers), there are two plausible explanations. The first focuses on fear: namely, North Korea's fear that, having frozen its plutonium-based nuclear program in 1994, it would receive nothing in return. Such a suspicion seems unreasonable on its face, since, under the 1994 Agreed Framework negotiated with Washington, Pyongyang was to be compensated in various ways for abandoning its nuclear ambitions. But from the perspective of a paranoid, isolated regime such as North Korea's, this concern was not without justification. Almost from its inception, the provisions of the 1994 accord fell substantially behind schedule—most notably in the construction of proliferation-resistant light-water reactors in the North and improved relations with the United States. North Korea may thus have started its HEU program as a hedge against the possibility that it had been duped, or, more likely, that new U.S., South Korean, or Japanese administrations would be less willing to proceed with the politically controversial program than were their predecessors.

> *The 1994 Agreed Framework, although deeply flawed, represented the best deal available at a far from ideal time.*

A second, darker, and more likely explanation for Pyongyang's decision to start the HEU program holds that the North never really intended to give up its nuclear ambitions. Whether motivated by fear, honor, or aggression (the determination to stage a preemptive strike if threatened), Pyongyang views a nuclear program as its sovereign right—and a necessity.

Whichever of these theories is true, the North seems to have undertaken its HEU program slowly at first, ramping it up only in late 2000 or 2001. And it was able to hide the program until July 2002, when U.S. intelligence proved its existence. Although Bush administration officials insist otherwise, it is possible, as North Korean officials have suggested, that Pyongyang decided to step up its nuclear program in response to what it perceived as Washington's increasingly hostile attitude—a hostility demonstrated to North Koreans by President Bush's decision to include them in the "axis of evil" and to set the bar for talks impossibly high. This perceived hostility was further encouraged when the administration announced its new doctrine of pre-emptive defense. Notwithstanding the president's remarks to the contrary, Pyongyang views the new defense doctrine as a direct threat. After all, if Washington is willing to attack Iraq, another isolated nation with a suspected nuclear program, might it not also be willing, even likely, to do the same to North Korea?

This fear helps explain why the North decided to restart its plutonium program. Many within the senior ranks of the North Korean military believe that if the United States attacks, Pyongyang's position will be strengthened immeasurably by the possession of several nuclear weapons. North Korean planners thus reason that they should develop such weapons as quickly as possible, prior to the American attack that may come once Washington has concluded its war with Iraq.

North Korea's gamble

There are again two plausible explanations for why the North revealed its HEU program in October 2002. Since its earliest days in office, the Bush administration has made clear that it favors a more hard-line approach to North Korea than did the Clinton team. Even prior to the North's HEU admission, Bush's support for the 1994 Agreed Framework was lukewarm at best. His administration considered the accord a form of blackmail signed by his predecessor—even though, after a long review of North Korea policy in 2001, the Bush administration found it could not justify abandoning the pact without having something better with which to replace it. In short, Washington grudgingly considered itself bound by a diplomatic process it viewed as distasteful—if not an outright scam.

When U.S. Assistant Secretary of State James Kelly visited North Korea in early October, he took with him undeniable evidence of the North's HEU program. He also took with him very narrowly defined briefing papers, hard-line marching orders that reflected the influence of the Defense Department and the National Security Council.

Anticipating isolation and a worsening of already strained relations in the face of Washington's evidence, Pyongyang opted to play one of its few remaining trump cards: open admission of its nuclear program. This openness, Kim may have hoped, would keep the Bush administration from disengaging entirely. By acknowledging its HEU effort, Pyongyang essentially sent Washington the following message: "We understand that despite everything we've done over the past several months you want to isolate or disengage from us. Well, we admit we have a uranium-based nuclear program. You say you don't want to deal with us. Too bad—you can't ignore a potential nuclear power. Deal with us."

> *The timing of the steps now taken to resolve the current crisis will be crucial to their success.*

Another hypothesis to explain the timing is that Pyongyang simply miscalculated. North Korea watchers learned long ago to expect the unexpected, but even the most jaded observers were surprised in September 2002 when Kim admitted to [Japanese prime minister Junichiro] Koizumi that the North had abducted 13 Japanese in the 1970s and 1980s to train its spies. Kim apologized for the abductions and, with remarkable speed, subsequently authorized a visit of five of the surviving abductees to Japan. In doing so, he removed a decades-old barrier to normalization of relations between the two nations (and to the payment of billions of dollars in hoped-for war reparations from Tokyo).

Kim's gamble on coming clean about the abductions appeared at the time to have paid off. Notwithstanding the predicted public backlash in Japan, further talks between Tokyo and Pyongyang took place in October (after the HEU admission). Having experienced better-than-expected results in admitting to the abductions, Kim may have hoped for the same by confessing to his HEU program. His thinking may have been that, in view of Washington's evidence, Pyongyang would eventually have had to come clean anyway. That being the case, it was better to do so sooner rather than later, thereby removing one of the primary obstacles to improved U.S.-North Korea relations. Kim may further have surmised that the timing of such a revelation in October was advantageous, given recent progress in talks with Japan and South Korea. He probably hoped that Tokyo and Seoul would pressure Washington to mitigate its response.

In the weeks immediately following Kelly's visit, Washington made it clear that it did not see a military solution to the crisis on the Korean Peninsula. This left isolation, containment, and negotiation as the only viable alternatives. A policy of isolation would seek the North's collapse but would not address the HEU problem and would likely result in the North's restarting its plutonium-based nuclear program. Containment, or economic pressure designed to squeeze the North, would seek to punish Pyongyang while leaving the door open to future negotiation. It too would not address the HEU problem but, it was hoped, might maintain the freeze on the plutonium program. Negotiations, meanwhile, would seek to address the nuclear problem but could be viewed by some as a reward for bad behavior.

If a successful isolation or containment policy wins the day, the North will have miscalculated in coming clean. If, however, a policy of dialogue and subsequent negotiation ultimately emerges—or if isolation or containment fails (in part because Washington is unable to persuade China, South Korea, and Russia to endorse it over a sustained period)—Kim will have played his cards exceedingly well.

The benefits of the 1994 Agreed Framework

Many pundits and policymakers in Washington, on both sides of the aisle, argue that the revelations about Pyongyang's clandestine HEU program prove that President Clinton's policy of engaging the North was a mistake. This argument maintains that giving in to blackmail leads only to more blackmail.

Although it is inherently valid, such analysis is too simple. In 1994, the United States was on the edge of war with North Korea. Washington had beefed up its forces in the theater, installed Patriot missile batteries in the South, and was reviewing detailed war plans. The White House had even begun to consider the evacuation of American citizens. The 1994 Agreed

Framework, although deeply flawed, represented the best deal available at a far from ideal time. It remained so for several years. And although it has been disappointing on many levels, the agreement has not been useless.

Indeed, it averted a potentially catastrophic situation. Instead of a war (which the U.S. military commander in South Korea, General Gary Luck, estimated would have killed a million people, including 80,000 to 100,000 Americans), Northeast Asia has experienced eight years of stability. This has had vast implications beyond security. In 1994, South Korea's GDP was 323 trillion won; today, even after the 1997 financial meltdown, its GDP is approximately 544 trillion won. This transformation would have been unlikely in the face of imminent armed conflict. China has similarly experienced explosive growth, much of which might also have slowed had there been a major confrontation on its porous border with North Korea.

> *At its core—politics stripped aside—the current standoff will allow Washington to scrap the flawed Agreed Framework and replace it with a new mechanism that better addresses the concerns of the United States and its allies.*

The Agreed Framework also provided the parties with critical breathing room, which has allowed new realities to emerge both within North Korea and among the United States and its allies—developments that improve the chances for a better, more comprehensive deal today. To cite one example, in 1994, Kim Jong Il had only recently succeeded his father, North Korea's founder Kim Il Sung. Viewed as weak, mentally unstable, and without a power base of his own, Kim was expected to last a mere two weeks to several months. Today, however, he is acknowledged as the only power in North Korea and has established diplomatic relations with scores of nations, including many of Washington's closest allies in NATO and the European Union. This puts him in a vastly better position to strike a deal.

For its part, the United States in 1994 could not have counted on Russia or China to support its position toward North Korea. Today, however, Washington is likely to receive baseline support—albeit not carte blanche—from both. Indeed, although there has hardly been unanimity among the outside powers, there has already been evidence of such cooperation, in the form of a joint Chinese-Russian declaration issued in early December [2002] stating that the two powers "consider it important . . . to preserve the non-nuclear status of the Korean Peninsula and the regime of non-proliferation of weapons of mass destruction."

Another benefit of the breathing room created by the 1994 accord is the North's economic dependence on the South. South Korea today is North Korea's largest publicly acknowledged supplier of aid and its second-largest trading partner. Although not as successful as he would have liked, former South Korean President Kim Dae Jung's "Sunshine Policy" of engaging the North has, in conjunction with the North's economic collapse, given Pyongyang a strong economic interest in avoiding a crisis. (Although the numbers are much smaller, the situation is not wholly unlike that between Taiwan and China.) Should the North exacerbate current tensions, the economic fallout would be traumatic, and the loss of South Korean investment could destabilize the North.

The importance of timing

The timing of the steps now taken to resolve the current crisis will be crucial to their success. Indeed, timing is important to understand because the North's HEU program does not pose an immediate threat. Although it has the potential to eventually produce enough uranium for one nuclear weapon per year, it has not yet reached this stage and is not expected to do so for at least two to three more years, according to administration officials and the Central Intelligence Agency.

The North's decision to reopen its plutonium-based nuclear program at Yongbyon poses a more critical and immediate threat, however. Prior to its suspension in 1994, most experts believe this program had already produced enough plutonium for one or two nuclear weapons. The 8,000 spent fuel rods from the five-megawatt reactor contained enough plutonium for an additional four to five nuclear weapons. The IAEA monitored the freeze via seals, cameras, and on-site inspectors. It also canned the 8,000 existing spent fuel rods, placed them in a safe-storage cooling pond, and monitored them until its inspectors were expelled from North Korea on December 31 [2002].

The five-megawatt reactor, when operational, will produce enough plutonium for one or two additional nuclear weapons per year. But the 8,000 rods represent an even more immediate challenge. If the North follows through on its threat to reopen the reprocessing facility in February, it would take just six months to reprocess all of its spent fuel and extract enough plutonium to make four or five additional weapons. This would bring Pyongyang's nuclear arsenal to between five and seven weapons by the end of July. It could have enough plutonium for one to three weapons even sooner.

> *Those who think they can outwait Pyongyang by isolating it or pressuring it economically, as the Bush administration proposed in late December, are likely to be proved wrong.*

Thus there exists only a short window of opportunity before the North's recent action translates into additional nuclear-weapons material on the ground. The trick to unraveling the current impasse is to avoid rewarding the North for its violations of past treaties with a new, more comprehensive agreement. Blackmail cannot and should not be condoned. The starting point for future discussions should therefore be that the North must completely and immediately abandon its HEU and plutonium-based programs. This pledge must be accompanied by intrusive, immediate, and continuous inspections by the IAEA.

Negotiating a new agreement with North Korea

It is a tenet of all international negotiations, however—particularly those that involve the Korean Peninsula—that all crises create opportunity, and this one is no different. At its core—politics stripped aside—the current standoff will allow Washington to scrap the flawed Agreed Framework and replace it with a new mechanism that better addresses the concerns of the United States and its allies. In many ways, the North's HEU admission and its subsequent decision to reopen its plutonium program might therefore be viewed as a blessing in disguise. The Bush administration can finally rid itself of a deal it never liked and never truly endorsed and replace it with one that addresses all of Washington's central concerns, including the North's missile program and its conventional forces. Washington must, however, be willing to make such a deal attractive to the North as well.

Yet timing poses an immediate barrier to negotiating a new mechanism. Pyongyang has insisted it will give up its HEU and plutonium programs only after Washington signs a nonaggression pact with it. But the Bush administration, while publicly reassuring the North that it has no intention of invading, has justifiably insisted that Pyongyang give up these programs before there is any discussion of a new mechanism. The North seems unwilling to lose face by giving up this trump card without a security guarantee, and Washington is unwilling to take any action that appears to reward Pyongyang before it has fully dismantled its nuclear programs.

Those who think they can outwait Pyongyang by isolating it or pressuring it economically, as the Bush administration proposed in late December [2002], are likely to be proved wrong. North Koreans are a fiercely proud people and have endured hardships over the last decade that would have led most other countries to implode. It would therefore be a mistake to underestimate their loyalty to the state or to Kim Jong Il. When insulted, provoked, or threatened, North Koreans will not hesitate to engage in their equivalent of a holy war. Their ideology is not only political, it is quasi-religious. Pyongyang also enjoys an inherent advantage in any waiting game: Beijing. Although China might initially support a policy of economic pressure, Beijing is afraid that it will face a massive influx of unwanted refugees across the Yalu River should the North collapse. To guard against this event, it will ultimately allow fuel and food (sanctioned or unsanctioned) to move across its border with the North. Similarly, South Korea, which also wants to avoid a massive influx of refugees, is unlikely to support a sustained, indefinite policy of squeezing the North. In mid-December [2002], it elected by a larger margin than predicted a new president who ran specifically on a platform of expanding engagement with Pyongyang.

A two-stage approach

The way to cut the Gordian knot of who goes first is through a two-stage approach. The first stage would provide the North with the security it craves while also ensuring that Pyongyang is not rewarded for its bad behavior. To achieve this end, the four outside interested powers (the United States, Japan, China, and Russia—each of which has supported one side or the other in the past) would jointly and officially guarantee the security and stability of the entire Korean Peninsula. Washington may not be able or willing to convene a meeting of the four powers to this end. If not, back channels or unofficial initiatives should be used to encourage Moscow or Beijing to take the lead. Both Russia and China have sought to increase their influence on the Korean Peninsula in recent years. This plan would solidify their places at the table.

> *Initially, Washington's response to North Korea's HEU and plutonium programs consisted mostly of condemning Pyongyang.*

Once the security of the peninsula has been guaranteed by the outside powers, it will be time for stage two: a comprehensive accord, again broken into two parts. The North must completely give up its HEU and plutonium programs and allow immediate, intrusive, and continuous inspections by the IAEA; end its development, production, and testing of long-range missiles in exchange for some financial compensation; draw down its conventional troops along the DMZ [demilitarized zone—the dividing line between North and South Korea] (although there will be no reduction of U.S. troops at this time, and only a very limited reduction of U.S. troops in five years, should the situation permit); and, finally, continue to implement economic and market reforms.

In exchange for the above, Japan would normalize its relations with the North within 18 months of the agreement's coming into effect. This normalization would include the payment of war reparations in the form of aid, delivered on a timetable extending five to seven years. Both halves of the peninsula would also enter a Korean federation within two years of the agreement's coming into effect. And as soon as the IAEA had verified that the North has dismantled its nuclear weapons programs, Washington would sign a nonaggression pact with Pyongyang. This pact, which by prior agreement would automatically be nullified by subsequent signs that the North was not cooperating or was initiating a new nuclear program, would include the gradual lifting of economic sanctions over three years.

The United States, South Korea, Japan, and the European Union—the primary members of the Korean Peninsula Energy Development Organization (or KEDO, which was set up to administer the Agreed Framework)—would further maintain the organization and provide the two new light-water reactors stipulated in the original deal. KEDO would also resume delivery of heavy fuel oil until the first reactor was completed.

In addition to the above measures, China and Russia would agree to support the North economically via investment. All outside parties to the deal—the United States, South Korea, Japan, China, and Russia—would also contribute to the compensation the North would receive in return for ending its long-range missile program.

Finally, five years after the above accord is signed, a Northeast Asia Security Forum, consisting of the four major powers plus South and North Korea, would be created to ensure long-term peace and stability throughout the region.

The timing of the various parts of stage two will be critical to its success. To this end, the leaders of all the countries involved (or their high-ranking representatives) should meet in person to negotiate the deal. North and South Korea, Japan, China, Russia, and the United States must all sign on if the plan is to work.

Certain components of the comprehensive deal (such as the U.S.-North Korea nonaggression pact and the missile accord) should exist as separate agreements, referenced in but not attached as appendices to the main text. They should be fully agreed [on] and initialed prior to signing the comprehensive deal. Immediately after signing the comprehensive agreement, the North would have to take the first step by fully dismantling both its HEU and its plutonium programs and allowing IAEA inspections to verify these steps. Only after the IAEA had certified the dismantling would the nonaggression and missile pacts be signed: in the case of the nonaggression pact, by Pyongyang and Washington alone, and in the case of the missile pact, by Beijing, Moscow, Pyongyang, Seoul, Tokyo, and Washington.

The United States must move forward toward resolution

Initially, Washington's response to North Korea's HEU and plutonium programs consisted mostly of condemning Pyongyang. Then, in early January [2003], President Bush and Secretary of State Powell took steps to ease the tension. Following a trilateral meeting with South Korea and Japan (during which Seoul and Tokyo pressed for a diplomatic approach), Washington finally agreed to open a dialogue with Pyongyang. The Bush administration, however, limited the scope of the meetings to discussion of how North Korea could abide by its international commitments. It is now time to move beyond this narrow agenda to a policy of resolution—one that addresses all concerns on the Korean Peninsula.

Such a shift is particularly important given the very serious rupture that has opened between Washington and Seoul. At precisely the time that the situation in North Korea has reached a crisis stage, U.S.–South Korean relations have hit their lowest level ever. Korean anti-Americanism—far more than just a difference of opinion on how to deal with the North—was responsible for the election of Roh Moo Hyun as president in December [2003]. Roh beat a more hard-line rival specifically by distancing himself from Washington's position on the North and by promising to continue Kim Dae Jung's Sunshine Policy. More critically, he promised a new, more prominent role for South Korea in its relationship with the United States. America will therefore no longer be able to force its position on the more assertive and restless South Korean population.

The process above, fortunately, will address the major concerns of all the parties involved. It will assure North Korea of the underlying security it seeks, without requiring Washington to sign a nonaggression pact until after Pyongyang has dismantled its HEU and plutonium programs. If the North balks despite a security guarantee by all major outside powers and the prospect of a comprehensive accord, isolation or economic pressure by Washington and its allies will not only remain a viable alternative, it will be stronger and more fully justified than it would be otherwise, and will more easily win the unified, sustained support of major players in the region. The upside to exploring the path presented above is therefore massive, and the downside very limited. Doing nothing, meanwhile, could become the most dangerous option of all.

13

The United States Must Use Diplomacy to End North Korea's Nuclear Program

Nina Hachigian

Nina Hachigian is a senior political scientist and director of the Center for Asia Pacific Policy at the RAND Corporation.

The North Korean regime, not its weapons program, is the real cause of tension on the Korean Peninsula. Stability will therefore not be possible until the government of North Korea changes. However, the United States must separate its long-term goal of regime change from the need to resolve the immediate crisis of North Korea's resumption of nuclear weapons development. A successful resolution to this crisis requires diplomacy, and the United States should pursue negotiations wholeheartedly, even if talks prove difficult. The stakes are high: If the United States does not halt the North's nuclear program soon, the long-term U.S. goal of a stable, secure peninsula will be threatened.

Responding to China's overtures, North Korea has [in August 2003] agreed to a new round of multilateral talks on its claimed nuclear-weapons program. It is the nature of the North Korean regime itself, though, not the weapons program, that is the underlying cause of tension on the Korean peninsula.

The peninsula will never be truly politically and economically stable until there is radical change in the government of

Nina Hachigian, "US: Stick to Diplomacy with North Korea, Even If Talks Fail," *Christian Science Monitor*, August 7, 2003. Copyright © 2003 by Nina Hachigian. Reproduced by permission.

North Korea, either through unprecedented internal reform and opening, or through collapse of the regime. A government as isolated, economically backward, and repressive as North Korea's cannot exist peacefully in the modern world.

Because Kim Jong Il's government has no mandate and no legitimacy, it will always and necessarily act in unpredictable, destabilizing ways to preserve its own power.

> *The peninsula will never be truly politically and economically stable until there is radical change in the government of North Korea, either through unprecedented internal reform and opening, or through collapse of the regime.*

But we must separate our short-term needs from the long-term vision. To resolve the immediate problem of the North's nuclear program, diplomacy is the only path, and the US should pursue it wholeheartedly, despite its inherent messiness and difficulty. Though a breakthrough at the next round of talks should not be expected, negotiations with North Korea can work because each side clearly wants something. The North Koreans want aid and a security guarantee; the US, South Korea, China, Japan, Russia and Australia are united in demanding a Korean peninsula free of nuclear weapons. Reaching a compromise will not be easy, but it is far from impossible.

Economic pressures will not work

If talks fail to produce visible progress, there are some inside (and outside) the Bush administration who will renew their calls for a strategy of economic pressures instead of diplomacy. They have argued that a better government in North Korea is the right goal, and that measures the United States can take to hasten that end are all to the good. They advocate a short-term strategy of increased economic pressures—such as drug-sale interdictions recently carried out by Australia to stop illegal sources of cash, inspections of North Korean ships for illegal weapons by Japan, and even some form of blockade—that fits a broader strategy of isolating and undermining the government in Pyongyang.

This approach confuses the short- and long-term problems. As a complement to sincere, rigorous and determined diplomacy, such economic measures can demonstrate that the US and its partners are very serious and that the consequences of not reaching a deal will be severe. But without continuing talks, ratcheting up economic pressure would dangerously compromise our urgent short-term goal of halting North Korea's nascent nuclear program.

South Korea and China are unlikely to agree to using economic pressure on the North without a diplomatic counterpoint, and these two nations must agree for the plan to work. China supplies more than 70 percent of the North's fuel, and China and South Korea both send food and other needed goods.

For South Korea and China, a gradual, peaceful reunification of the two Koreas through increased engagement is the favored course. Reunification will pose a huge economic burden for South Korea that will only increase if it is not carefully orchestrated over a long period. Similarly, China has to worry about precipitating a refugee crisis.

> *To resolve the immediate problem of the North's nuclear program, diplomacy is the only path, and the US should pursue it wholeheartedly, despite its inherent messiness and difficulty.*

Moreover, Chinese and South Koreans have asserted, economic pressure is unlikely to have the desired effect of forcing the North to end its weapons program. *Juche*, or self-reliance, is the proclaimed national ideology, and North Korea has survived under dire economic conditions for decades. If anything, South Korea and China argue, economic pressure will only serve to harden the North's position that it must have a nuclear weapons program to protect it from hostile forces.

Urgent action is needed

The second problem with the strategy of an economic squeeze is that we do not have time to wait for it to work. Adding to the urgency is recent intelligence from South Korea suggesting there may be a second site other than Yongbyon at which

North Korea is reprocessing spent fuel rods. If the US does not halt the North's nuclear program in the short term, it will also compromise the long-term goal of a stable, secure peninsula. If North Korea's program continues unabated, it could have between four and 20 nuclear weapons by the end of the year and the ability to build perhaps four to six a year within two years.

With a full-blown nuclear program, the regime in Pyongyang [North Korea's capital] could sustain itself by selling nukes—to terrorist groups in the worst-case scenario. A nuclear North Korea could also spark a new arms race in East Asia. And no matter how we wish it to be otherwise, a nuclear-weapons program would give North Korea a perverse stature. Moreover, such a program would make securing nuclear materials after reunification greatly more challenging, as Russia watchers well know.

A better government in Pyongyang is a long-term vision. Stopping North Korea's nuclear program is a short-term necessity. Without rigorous and sustained diplomatic engagement, the chances are slim that we will achieve that necessary goal.

14

The United States Must Test Whether North Korea Is Willing to Negotiate

Joseph Cirincione and Jon Wolfsthal

Joseph Cirincione is the director and Jon Wolfsthal the deputy director of the Non-Proliferation Project at the Carnegie Endowment for International Peace.

Despite years of negotiations, threats, confrontations, and analysis, the United States still does not know whether North Korea is truly willing to negotiate a verifiable end to its nuclear weapons program. The United States should test North Korea's willingness to negotiate by establishing an ongoing negotiating plan that involves the six interested nations (North Korea, the United States, China, South Korea, Japan, and Russia), appointing a high-level presidential envoy to carry out the talks, communicating a clear U.S. position that has been agreed to in advance by Japan and South Korea, and continuing to encourage Chinese involvement. Finally, the United States must decide exactly what it is prepared to offer North Korea to terminate its nuclear program. If North Korea does not agree to negotiations, the United States can then consider punitive options such as military action, trade blockades, or other economic sanctions.

That North Korea is capable of building nuclear weapons is no longer in doubt. What remains unknown and what must be

Joseph Cirincione and Jon Wolfsthal, "Dealing with North Korea," *Carnegie Endowment for International Peace*, vol. 6, December 18, 2003. Copyright © 2003 by *Carnegie Endowment for International Peace*, Washington DC, www.ceip.org. Reproduced by permission.

addressed is the willingness of North Korea to negotiate a verifiable end to its nuclear weapons program. Despite more than 10 years of direct and indirect negotiations, threats, confrontations, and analysis, the United States still does not know with any certainty the answer to the question: Will North Korea verifiably eliminate all of its nuclear capabilities if the terms are right?

The United States must get serious in negotiations

There is clear and compelling evidence to support speculation on both sides, but neither case is conclusive. Yes, North Korea cheated on its agreements in the 1990s to freeze its nuclear activities, but it is equally true that during the 1990s the United States abandoned its efforts to normalize relations and improve ties with the North. The debate is not whether North Korea can be trusted; it clearly cannot. But can Pyongyang [the capital of North Korea] be motivated to abandon its nuclear program under effective inspections and, if not, what can outside states do about it?

> *What remains unknown and what must be addressed is the willingness of North Korea to negotiate a verifiable end to its nuclear weapons program.*

When North Korea's nuclear program was still in its infancy, the United States, South Korea, Japan, and others could afford to wait to answer these questions. Now that the North's program has come of age, they cannot. In a worst-case scenario, North Korea could produce more than 100 nuclear weapons by the end of the decade. Such an arsenal not only threatens U.S. allies and troops in the region, but given North Korea's economic strains, it is conceivable that it could sell nuclear materials to other states or even terrorist groups if the price is right. Such a scenario is so grave that U.S. policymakers could soon face a truly appalling choice between accepting its realization or plunging into a full-fledged war on the Korean peninsula. By comparison, many negotiated settlements—no matter how distasteful—become attractive.

It is time for the United States to get serious about negotiations with the North. The postponement of talks originally slated for this month [December 2003] are the latest sign that the Bush administration's approach to this critical issue has failed and that a new policy is needed. President George W. Bush's October statement that he is willing to consider some form of security guarantees for North Korea was a positive step in this direction, but the refusal to consider possible incentives for the North's abandonment of its program continues to sabotage any real progress. There is enough collective experience in the United States after 10 years of efforts to know how the North negotiates and how to make progress. At a minimum, it takes time and a complex mixture of resolve and open respect for the negotiations themselves. Any mixed messages, public or otherwise, can quickly derail progress and undercut efforts at negotiations.

Negotiation steps

To test whether North Korea is prepared to eliminate its program under effective verification, the United States needs to:

- Establish a full-time and ongoing negotiating mechanism based on the six-party talks. They should be continuous and establish a timeline for conclusion.
- Appoint higher-level representation for the talks, including a presidentially appointed envoy. This person must speak directly for the President, lead the negotiations and be prepared and empowered to make serious progress.
- Ensure continued presidential engagement with the negotiating process and effectively impose a coordinated position in the administration (no loose statements or diatribes).
- Maintain a common US, Japan, and South Korea position on the talks.
- Continue to encourage Chinese engagement, with the awareness of the limits of Chinese influence over North Korea.

Lastly, the Bush administration needs to determine what, if anything, it is prepared to offer North Korea if they terminate their nuclear program and eliminate, under effective verification, its nuclear capability. This can involve a broad mix of political, diplomatic, economic, and symbolic steps including establishment of diplomatic relations and the provision of considerable agricultural assistance. Even if the administration is now prepared to test North's Korea's willingness to give up its program, as long as the debate over possible inducements continues, progress will be all but impossible to the detriment of US security.

Moreover, the United States should be prepared to offer more to get more. The nuclear issue is so pressing, however, that it should not become hostage to issues related to ballistic missiles, conventional force deployments, chemical and biological weapon programs, and human rights. The United States should work to resolve those issues but only once the nuclear question is answered.

President Bush has moved from a wholesale rejection of negotiations with the North to the verge of a new set of real talks. To make progress, he must take the next step: test North Korea directly and conclusively. If a positive result materializes, the president must be willing to invest his personal prestige domestically and abroad to make the deal stick. If the result is negative, having tried the alternative, punitive options will remain viable, and he will have created broader support for confronting North Korea's continued pursuit of nuclear weapons.

Organizations to Contact

The editors have compiled the following list of organizations concerned with the issues debated in this book. The descriptions are derived from materials provided by the organizations. All have publications or information available for interested readers. The list was compiled on the date of publication of the present volume; the information provided here may change. Be aware that many organizations take several weeks or longer to respond to inquiries, so allow as much time as possible.

American Enterprise Institute
1150 Seventeenth St. NW, Washington, DC 20036
(202) 862-5800 • fax: (202) 862-7177
e-mail: info@aei.org • Web site: www.aei.org

The American Enterprise Institute, founded in 1943, is one of America's largest think tanks. It is dedicated to preserving and strengthening the foundations of freedom—limited government, private enterprise, vital cultural and political institutions, and a strong foreign policy and national defense—through scholarly research, open debate, and publications. Its Web site contains various articles on the North Korean situation.

Brookings Institution
1775 Massachusetts Ave. NW, Washington, DC 20036
(202) 797-6000 • fax: (202) 797-6004
e-mail: brookinfo@brook.edu • Web site: www.brook.edu

The Brookings Institution is an independent, nonpartisan organization devoted to research, analysis, education, and publication focused on public policy issues in the areas of economics, foreign policy, and governance. The goal of Brookings activities is to improve the performance of American institutions and the quality of public policy by using social science to analyze emerging issues and to offer practical approaches to those issues in language aimed at the general public. Brookings publishes the *Brookings Review* quarterly as well as numerous books and articles on foreign policy issues such as the North Korean nuclear issue.

Carnegie Endowment for International Peace
1779 Massachusetts Ave. NW, Washington, DC 20036-2103
(202) 483-7600 • fax: (202) 483-1840
e-mail: info@ceip.org • Web site: www.ceip.org

The Carnegie Endowment for International Peace is a private nonprofit organization dedicated to advancing cooperation between nations and promoting active international engagement by the United States. Founded in 1910, its work is nonpartisan and dedicated to achieving practical results through research, publishing, convening, and on occasion, creating new institutions and international networks. The Carnegie Endowment publishes *Foreign Policy*, one of the world's leading magazines of international politics and economics. Many articles, issue briefs, and other materials concerning North Korea can be found on the endowment's Web site.

The Cato Institute
1000 Massachusetts Ave. NW, Washington, DC 20001-5403
(202) 842-0200 • fax: (202) 842-3490
Web site: www.cato.org

The Cato Institute is a libertarian public policy research foundation that seeks to broaden the parameters of public policy debate to allow consideration of the principles of limited government, individual liberty, free markets, and peace. Toward that goal, the institute strives to achieve greater involvement of the intelligent, concerned lay public in questions of policy and the proper role of government. The institute has an extensive publications program that offers books, monographs, briefing papers, and shorter studies on various issues, including North Korea.

Center for Strategic and International Studies (CSIS)
1800 K St. NW, Washington, DC 20006
(202) 887-0200 • fax: (202) 775-3199
e-mail: webmaster@csis.org • Web site: www.csis.org

The Center for Strategic and International Studies is a private, nonpartisan, and tax-exempt organization dedicated to providing world leaders with strategic insights on—and policy solutions to—current and emerging global issues. CSIS is led by John J. Hamre, formerly deputy secretary of defense, and guided by a board of trustees chaired by former senator Sam Nunn and consisting of prominent individuals from both the public and private sectors. The CSIS staff focus primarily on three subject areas: challenges to national and international security, the world's major geographical regions, and issues concerning methods of governance for the global age. To this end, CSIS has programs on technology and public policy, international trade and finance, and energy. The center's Web site contains numerous articles on the North Korean crisis.

Council on Foreign Relations
1779 Massachusetts Ave. NW, Washington, DC 20036
(202) 518-3400 • fax: (202) 986-2984
e-mail: communications@cfr.org • Web site: www.cfr.org

Founded in 1921, the Council on Foreign Relations is an independent, national membership organization and a nonpartisan center for scholars dedicated to producing and disseminating ideas so that individual and corporate members, as well as policy makers, journalists, students, and interested citizens in the United States and other countries, can better understand the world and the foreign policy choices facing the United States and other governments. The council publishes a highly respected journal titled *Foreign Affairs*, and articles on nuclear proliferation and the North Korean nuclear crisis are available on the council's Web site.

Federation of American Scientists
1717 K St. NW, Suite 209, Washington, DC 20036
(202) 546-3300 • fax: (202) 675-1010
e-mail: fas@fas.org • Web site: www.fas.org

The Federation of American Scientists was founded as a nonprofit organization in 1945 by members of the Manhattan Project, creators of the atom bomb. Its focus is the implications of nuclear power and weaponry for the future of humankind and its Web site contains information about North Korea's nuclear program.

Foreign Policy in Focus (FPIF)
733 Fifteenth St. NW, Suite 1020, Washington, DC, 20005
(202) 234-9382
Web site: www.fpif.org

Foreign Policy in Focus was established in 1996 as a collaborative project of the Interhemispheric Resource Center (IRC) and the Institute for Policy Studies (IPS). It is a "think tank without walls" that functions as an international network of more than 650 policy analysts and advocates. Unlike traditional think tanks, FPIF is committed to advancing a citizen-based foreign policy agenda—one that is fundamentally rooted in citizen initiatives and movements. Publications on North Korea can be found on FPIF's Web site.

Institute for Policy Studies (IPS)
733 Fifteenth St. NW, Suite 1020, Washington, DC 20005
(202) 234-9382 • fax: (202) 387-7915
Web site: www.ips-dc.org

The Institute for Policy Studies is the nation's oldest multi-issue progressive think tank. Based in Washington, D.C., but with links to activists and scholars across the nation and around the world, the institute serves as a bridge between progressive forces in government and grassroots activists, and between movements in the United States and those in the developing world. Its Web site lists books and reports available from the institute.

RAND Corporation
PO Box 2138, 1700 Main St., Santa Monica, CA 90407-2138
(310) 393-0411
e-mail: correspondence@rand.org • Web site: www.rand.org

The RAND Corporation is a nonprofit research organization providing analysis and solutions to address the challenges facing the public and private sectors around the world. The RAND Corporation has pursued its nonprofit mission by conducting research on important and complicated problems in areas such as national security, business, education, health, law, and science. The RAND Corporation publishes books and other publications, and its Web site offers articles on issues involving North Korea.

Bibliography

Books

Tsuneo Akaha · *The Future of North Korea*. New York: Routledge, 2002.

D. Ellsworth Blanc, ed. · *North Korea: Pariah?* Huntington, NY: Novinka Books, 2001.

Adrian Buzo · *The Guerilla Dynasty*. Boulder, CO: Westview, 1999.

Adrian Buzo · *The Making of Modern Korea*. New York: Routledge, 2002.

Victor D. Cha and David C. Kang · *Nuclear North Korea: A Debate on Engagement Strategies*. New York: Columbia University Press, 2003.

Chuck Downs · *Over the Line: North Korea's Negotiating Strategy*. Washington, DC: AEI Press, 1999.

Alexandra Kura · *Rogue Countries: Background and Current Issues*. Huntington, NY: Nova Science, 2001.

Andrew Mack · *Nuclear Endgame on the Korean Peninsula*. Canberra, Australia: Research School of Pacific Studies, Australian National University, 1994.

Andrea Matles Savada, ed. · *North Korea: A Country Study*. Washington, DC: U.S. Government Printing Office, 1994.

Han S. Park · *North Korea: The Politics of Unconventional Wisdom*. Boulder, CO: Lynne Rienner, 2002.

Leon V. Sigal · *Disarming Strangers: Nuclear Diplomacy with North Korea*. Princeton, NJ: Princeton University Press, 1998.

Dae Sook Suh and Chae-Jin Lee · *North Korea After Kim Il Sung*. Boulder, CO: Lynne Rienner, 1998.

Periodicals

Yinhay Ahn · "North Korea in 2001: At a Crossroads," *Asian Survey*, January/February 2002.

David Albright and Holly Higgins · "North Korea: It's Taking Too Long: Inspections in North Korea Are Tied to the Reactor Deal, Which Is Far Behind Schedule," *Bulletin of the Atomic Scientists*, January/February 2002.

Massimo Calabresi   "The Next WMD Crisis: New Evidence Suggests
                        North Korea Is Advancing Its Nuclear-Weapons
                        Plans. What Can the U.S. Do?" *Time*, July 28,
                        2003.

Victor D. Cha   "North Korea's Weapons of Mass Destruction:
                        Badges, Shields, or Swords?" *Political Science Quarterly*, Summer 2002.

Bruce Cumings   "Endgame in Korea," *Nation*, November 18, 2002.

Economist   "Getting the Genie Back into the Bottle: North Korea's Nuclear Programme," October 24, 2002.

Kristen Eichensehr   "Broken Promises," *Harvard International Review*,
                        Fall 2001.

Adam Garfinkle   "Checking Kim: The Awful Question of What to
                        Do," *National Review*, January 27, 2003.

Adam Garfinkle   "Power Play—How to Overthrow Pyongyang—
                        Peacefully," *New Republic*, November 4, 2002.

Philip Gourevitch   "Alone in the Dark," *New Yorker*, September 8,
                        2003.

Thomas H. Henrikson   "The Rise and Decline of Rogue States," *Vital
                        Speeches*, March 1, 2001.

Paul Kerr   "U.S. Courts Allies to Contain North Korea, Talks
                        Lag," *Arms Control Today*, July/August 2003.

Daryl G. Kimball   "Course Correction on North Korea," *Arms Control
                        Today*, November 2003.

Adriana S. Lee   "Secret Lives: For Two Decades, Sung Hae Rang
                        Lived Behind Closed Doors with the Despot Said
                        to Be the World's Most Dangerous Madman," *Time
                        International*, June 30, 2003.

National Review   "North Korea: Proliferation," November 11, 2002.

Michael O'Hanlon   "Economic Reform and Military Downsizing:
and Mike Mochizuki   A Key to Solving the North Korean Nuclear Crisis,"
                        Brookings Review, Fall 2003.

Thomas Omestad   "North Korea Breaks a No-Nukes Deal," *U.S. News
and Mark Mazzetti   & World Report*, October 28, 2002.

Bill Powell   "Nuclear Blackmail: North Korea Is No Iraq.
                        There's No Military Option. So How Do You Get a
                        Defiant Kim Jong Il to Give Up His Nukes?" *Fortune*, January 20, 2003.

Progressive   "Axis to Grind," March 2002.

Sharif Shuja   "North Korea and the Nuclear Threat," *Contemporary Review*, May 2003.

Jonathan Watts   "Balancing the 'Axis of Evil' in Northeast Asia,"
                        Lancet, September 7, 2002.

George Wehrfritz   "The Chinese Puzzle: Kim Jong Il Says He Has the
                          Bomb. Beijing Is Key to Making Him Give It Up,"
                          Newsweek, May 5, 2003.

Web Sites

Korean News Service (www.kcna.co.jp). This is the Web site for the Korean
Central News Agency, a state-run agency of the Democratic People's Republic of Korea. It speaks for the Workers' Party of Korea and the DPRK
government.

Korea Web Weekly (www.kimsoft.com). This is a Web site on all things
Korean. It includes information on history, culture, economy, politics and
military.

Index